Padre George Smith
of
Rorke's Drift

By the same Author
Be Prepared (1916)
The Roll of the Victoria Cross (1925)
*The County March of the 2nd Battalion
 The Suffolk Regiment* (1927)
History of Coddenham - MS., 2 vols (1931 and 1977)
Kesgrave: Church and Parish (1937)
The Churches of Bungay (1950)
Honour of the Light Brigade (1974)
*John Howes of Windham(*1976*)*
V.C. and G.C. Biographies - MSS. (1956-1977)

Editorships
The XI Hussar Journal (1911-13)
The Suffolk Regimental Gazette
Kesgrave Parish Magazine (1933-41)
Bungay Parish Magazine (1941-58)

Frontispiece

The Reverend George Smith, C.F.

Padre George Smith
of
Rorke's Drift

by Canon William M. Lummis, M.C.

Published for Canon William M. Lummis
by Wensum Books (Norwich) Ltd
4 Farmers Avenue
Norwich

First published February 1978
1SBN 0 903619 21 0
© Canon William M. Lummis 1978

Printed by Euromedia Print Ltd
Norwich
Bound by Hunter & Foulis Ltd
Edinburgh

Contents

List of Illustrations

Foreword

William Lummis, to whose dedicated and enthusiastic research we owe this book, has always had two great loves in his long life—the Army and the Church. He enlisted in the 11th Hussars at Colchester as far back as 9 June 1904. He was commissioned in the 2nd Battalion of the Suffolk Regiment in 1916 and continued to serve until he retired as Captain in 1930. He then started his second career and was ordained deacon in St Matthew's Church, Ipswich by the Bishop of St Edmundsbury and Ipswich on 21 December of that same year. He became Vicar of Kesgrave three years later and in 1941 began his long and memorable ministry in the town of Bungay, a ministry which lasted until his retirement in 1958, and is still remembered with thankfulness and affection twenty years later.

These two great interests in his life are fused in this delightful book in which Canon Lummis gives us a fascinating picture of Padre George Smith of Rorke's Drift. This brave son of Norfolk went out as a missionary to Zululand in 1872 and was then caught up inadvertently with the Zulu wars. He was appointed an Army Chaplain as a result of his services to the Forces of the Queen at the Battle of Rorke's Drift and remained a chaplain for the next twenty-five years.

Canon Lummis gives us a fascinating picture of this 'big red-bearded Norfolk giant' and we get an insight into the life and character of a man of great kindness and compassion, but who was as keen on a fight as any of his fellow soldiers. All those who thrill to the adventurous spirit of our forefathers and Norfolk people in particular will find this book a sheer delight.

The Right Reverend Aubrey Aitken, D.D.
Bishop of Lynn

Introduction
and Acknowledgements

Sir H. Rider Haggard in his account of Rorke's Drift which appeared in *The True Story Book*, edited by Andrew Melville, described George Smith as being a 'big red-bearded Norfolk giant', but did not give his place of birth. I was determined to discover this fact; but there are seven hundred civil parishes in Norfolk, and to trace the right George Smith seemed an almost impossible task.

My first clue, after many years, came from Lieutenant-Colonel G. G. E. Crew, the Warden and Curator of the Museum of the Royal Army Chaplains Department Headquarters at Bagshot Park, Surrey, former residence of H.R.H. The Duke of Connaught. He kindly lent me a copy of the *Royal Army Chaplains Department Journal* for July 1936. Inside was an account of the Reverend George Smith's Chaplaincy at Fulwood Barracks, Preston, together with the Diary he wrote of his experiences at Rorke's Drift, and his obituary written by G. V. Riley. I am indebted to the Chaplain-General to the Forces for his kind permission to include these items in my book. I am also extremely grateful to Colonel Crew for lending me the coloured portrait of the Reverend George Smith, C.F., which I first saw in the Museum at Bagshot Park, and which appears as the frontispiece. I have to apologize to him for the long interval of time which unfortunately elapsed before the framed portrait was restored to the Museum.

The jacket illustrates Padre George Smith distributing ammunition to the men of the 2nd Battalion of the 24th Regiment defending Rorke's Drift and Corporal Schiess, the

Swiss V.C., who is seen bayoneting Zulus. This picture is a detail of the painting by De Neuville of the Defence of Rorke's Drift, the original of which is in the Africana Museum, Johannesburg. This picture also appears in *For Valour - The History of South Africa's Victoria Cross Heroes* by Ian S. Uys where my friend Ian has wrongly described the Chaplain as Commissary Dunn. I am indebted to Ian for the photograph of the Eyebrow Hill on page 48.

Mr Donald R. Morris has graciously given me permission to quote from his most comprehensive book *The Washing of the Spears*.

Mr Richard F. Watson, F.L.A., District Librarian, Preston, has provided me with extracts from the *Preston Guardian* and the *Lancashire Daily Post* giving accounts of George Smith's funeral, and Mr J. Hodgson of Preston, the account of his death also in the *Lancashire Daily Post*. Mr Hodgson has also presented me with the photograph he took of the Reverend George Smith's grave in Preston Cemetery.

More information was obtained from a booklet entitled *The King's Division Depot, Lancashire, The Garrison Church of St. Alban, Fulwood Barracks*, a copy of which was sent to me by Major P. Mauldon, Curator of the Museum at Regimental Headquarters, The Queen's Lancashire Regiment, Fulwood Barracks, Preston.

Crockford's Clerical Directory, 1917, contains an account of George Smith's services as a missionary and as Chaplain to the Forces.

My son, Lieutenant-Colonel Eric T. Lummis, The Suffolk Regiment (retired), now a Principal Officer in the Department of the Environment, provided me with an extract from the Diary of G. L. Massy of the 94th Foot dealing with George Smith.

The mystery of George Smith's birthplace was cleared up by the account of his death in the *Lancashire Daily Post*, which stated that he was a native of Docking in Norfolk.

Approaching the Vicar of Docking, the Reverend Robert Tomlinson, I obtained from him the date of George's baptism — 9 January 1845. Naturally I supposed that he was born during the previous quarter, and sure enough a certificate of birth was obtained from the Registrar-General giving a date in

December 1844, but it was pointed out that his father was not a shoemaker and, therefore, not the George Smith the subject of this book. Fortunately, a second application produced a certificate that our George Smith was born on 8 January 1845.

Mr Gerald Hagan in his book *Dry Docking* makes one reference to George Smith giving information to Canon H. J. Hare, as to the dates of the Church Plate, but misses the interesting fact that he was one of the national heroes who had been born in the parish.

My greatest thanks I feel must be accorded to Mrs Brenda Hough, Archivist of the Headquarters of the Universities' Society for the Propagation of the Gospel, who allowed me to make several days' search of the reports of George Smith and other missionaries in Zululand, from 1872 to 1879, and also kindly provided me with a photograph of George Smith's little Church of St John the Evangelist, Weston, and with photostats of papers published in *The Natal Government Gazette* of 6 April 1875, dealing with the rebellion of Langalibalele, sent to Headquarters by George Smith.

Finally, I am extremely grateful to the Bishop of Lynn for so kindly writing the Foreword.

Wm. M. LUMMIS

Wymondham, Norfolk

Chapter One

Early Life

The Baptismal Register of St Mary's Church, Docking, Norfolk records:

> Baptized January 9th, 1845, GEORGE, son of William and Francis [*sic*] Smith. Abode: Docking. Trade: Shoemaker. Ceremony performed by F. T. Hare, Curate.

Also recorded are the dates of birth and baptism of his brother William, born on 17 May 1838 and baptized on 29 July; and of John baptized on 25 December 1842. The date of birth of their father, William Smith, is uncertain, for there were two of this name. One, son of William and Alice Smith, born on 14 September 1801 and baptized in 1802; and the other, son of Thomas and Sarah Smith, born on 19 February 1806 and baptized that same year.

George Smith[1] was born at Docking on 8 January 1845, and as he was baptized the very next day it would appear that he was a weak or sickly child. Nevertheless, he grew up to be a Norfolk giant, of good physique, and lived to a ripe old age.

Docking is situated on one of the highest points of Norfolk in the Hundred of Smithdon, near King's Lynn. It was known as 'Dry Docking' as far back as the time of James I, there being a scarcity of water in the village. However, there were deep wells of excellent cold water from which, as late as 1928, delivery was made at the rate of one penny per pail.

In his book *Dry Docking*, Mr Gerald Hagan records some famous persons either born in, or associated with, the village. One notable from a well-known Norfolk family was Sir

---

[1] There was another George Smith born in Docking in December 1844. He was possibly the son of the George Smith who was one of the Trustees appointed for the Methodist Church on 18 May 1860.

Henry Walpole. He was baptized in the Parish Church in 1558. He was converted to Roman Catholicism and became a Jesuit in 1584. A fluent linguist he was Chaplain to the Spanish Army in Flanders from 1589 to 1591. Landing at Bridlington in Yorkshire in 1593, he was arrested and imprisoned at York. Removed to the Tower of London in 1594 he was put on the rack no less than fourteen times. Fifteen months later he was taken back to York where on 5 April 1595, he was hanged, drawn and quartered at Knavesmire, just outside the city. He was canonized at the Vatican on 25 October 1970 as one of the Forty English Martyrs. Another notable was Sir William Hoste who was a great friend and admirer of Nelson. He was victorious in the naval Battle of Lissa in 1811. Finally, even Fletcher Christian, the leader of the mutiny on the *Bounty* is supposed to have had some connection with Docking. Only the Reverend George Smith is totally overlooked as a national hero. The one mention made of him is of his having given a list of Holy Communion vessels of the Parish Church to the Rector, the Reverend Canon Hugh Francis Hare, in a letter written 8 December 1910.

Of the boyhood of George Smith nothing seems to be known. He turns up in 1868, at the age of twenty-three, at St Augustine's College in Canterbury. Two years later he went out to South Africa as a Lay Missionary under the auspices of the Society for the Propagation of the Gospel. There he was ordained Deacon in 1871 and Priest in 1872, by the Right Reverend John William Colenso, Bishop of Maritzburg. The Bishop had formerly been Rector of the tiny parish of Forncett St Mary in Norfolk.

The best accounts of George Smith's activities as a zealous and enterprising missionary are to be found in the quarterly and half-yearly reports he sent to S.P.G. Headquarters in London, from 1872 to 1876, and after that year the reports of other missionaries.

Chapter Two

Missionary Zeal

The following extract taken from the Reverend George Smith's Report to the S.P.G. for the half-year ending December 1872 gives some basic statistics relating to his mission.

ESTCOURT

Mission commenced 1872. It consists of 3,000 square miles; population 1,150 Europeans, including Dutch Boers, and 34,000 Kaffirs. Church members 100.

Average attendance: Estcourt [?]; Weston, Mooi River, 30. Communicants: Estcourt, 16; Weston, 10.

A small infant mission and yet unfinished Church, St. John's, Weston, Mooi River.

A parsonage house at Estcourt and a school-church in course of erection.

The Church of Estcourt is co-extensive with the large county of Weenen.

On the West the Drakensberg Mountains separate it from the Orange Free State, and on the North it extends to six miles of Zululand. Ground elevation, some points more than 5,000 feet above sea-level. Healthy climate. Hilly, well watered, but the eastern parts hilly and nearly destitute of trees.

At midsummer 1873 George Smith reports:

ESTCOURT is on the main route from the coast to the interior of Africa, and to the Diamond Fields and Gold Fields. Along this route are the 'towns' of WESTON on the Mooi River, ESTCOURT (centre of the parish 20 miles North of Weston) on Bushman River, and COLENSO, on the Tugela, 22 miles North of Estcourt. WEENEN now almost deserted; while ESTCOURT bids fair to become an important place.

But Colonial townships are, after all, but centres of populated districts, and European inhabitants are found on outlying farms many miles apart, scattered through the length and breadth of the land.

Its population, 1,150 Europeans and 34,000 Kaffirs. In Estcourt itself there are not more than 50 European residents. The natives are as scattered as the Europeans, each family having a separate kraal. Several persons on every farm.

On July 17, 1872, the Church at Weston being completed, its consecration was performed by the Bishop of Maritzburg [Colenso], and dedicated to St. John the Evangelist.

In September, 1872, a building was commenced for a school-church which was completed and a service held on Sunday, May 4 1873.

At a Christmas ordination in 1872 George Smith had been admitted to Priest's Orders.

The privilege of partaking in Holy Eucharist was greatly prized by the widely scattered and hitherto few members of our church. Few in number; but people of all denominations are glad to avail themselves of the opportunity of worship afforded them by our Services. It is, of course, a matter for thankfulness that so many should join in the beautiful service of our Church; but that sometimes two or three only should remain to partake in the Holy Eucharist, out of a congregation of forty is much to be deplored. But it is the duty of the missionary prayerfully to sow the good seed, and the Lord of the Harvest will give the increase in His good time. Many of the people ride from a distance of from 8 to 15 miles to attend Church. One man brought his child a distance of 40 miles to be baptized.

He gives details of his residence and church in Weston.

Although my residence is situated in the centre of the district, there are no European residents residing more than 60 miles off, so that a great deal of one's time is taken up with long journeys to outlying places - a ride of 70 miles in one day being no extraordinary occurrence.

On page 4 I have mounted a photograph of my little Church of St. John the Evangelist.

Church of St John the Evangelist, Weston, Mooi River, 1873.

U.S.P.G.

Nearly twelve months have elapsed since its construction, and the only protection the building has is a very slight wooden fence which the droves of oxen are continually rubbing down. The consecrated graveyard which surrounds the church is unenclosed and the only fence which will keep out pigs and cattle is a stone wall; but this is so costly in construction that some time must elapse before we can raise the necessary funds; but when completed a parishioner has promised to plant the whole enclosure with choice shrubs and trees.

The view of the church will also show you that the little bell tower contains no bell, and a bell is much needed; but a still greater need is that of glass for the windows. The canvas which was stretched across the empty window frames as a temporary measure now hangs in tatters. Ordinary window glass would be destroyed by the first hail storm, and so we have to wait until farmers and friends supply us with the means of getting glass durable and strong.

One parishioner has presented a very nice stone font; another a dozen forms, and all undertake in subscribing for a little American organ which we find of great assistance in our semi-choral services.

The school-church of St. Matthew's, Estcourt, is simply an oblong red-brick building (40 feet by 20 feet) with iron roof and square windows. It looks painfully like a 'Little Bethel' at home does. But, its outward appearance is, I think, compensated for by a more ecclesiastical interior.

I spoke of the European population in the district as 1,150, but more than half are Dutch Boers, many of them unable to speak English.

A great obstruction to one's work arises from the unattractiveness of the Colony brought about by the Colenso difficulty. Colonists - even those who do not oppose us - will speak of our good Bishop of Maritzburg, his clergy and people, as members of the Church of South Africa, while they claim for Dr. Colenso, his ministers and followers, the sole right to be styled members of the Church of England.

It is most gratifying to find that many travelling miners and diggers, journeying to and from the Diamond and Gold Regions, avail themselves of the opportunity of attending Divine Service which the little roadside Temples afford them.

In March 1873 he had announced the installation of the American organ in St John's.

At this point a big change is about to take place in the life and experiences of this zealous missionary and the next report from him deserves another chapter.

Chapter Three

Native Rebellion

The report of March 1873 describes the situation at St
Matthew's, Estcourt.

At the present moment it is being turned into a Citadel, and a
laager or erection made in front of it with wagons. I will tell you
how this is.

There is a Native Chief, a very powerful one, named
Langalibalele,[1] living in the district. His people have many of
them working in the Diamond fields and, contrary to the Laws of
the Colony, they have most of them brought back guns and
ammunition with them. Of course if this sort of thing were
allowed, and the 33,300 natives within the Colony were to be
equipped with firearms, the 16,000 Europeans would be entirely
at their mercy.

Well, the Government have ordered the Chief to appear in
Maritzburg to explain his conduct and have the guns given up. He
has refused to appear. Again he has been summoned, but he has
now defied the Governor, taken away his fifty wives and his
thousands of heads of cattle, and he and his warriors have taken
refuge in lofty clefts of the precipitous range of the Drakensberg.

A detachment from the Regular Troops have left Maritzburg,
the main Volunteer Forces in the Colony are called out, some
thousands of loyal natives accompanying them, and probably this
display of force will overawe the rebellious old fellow and induce
him to surrender.

In the meantime, as I have already intimated, the residents
upon outlying farms thinking their security doubtful, although I
believe all fear is groundless, are bringing in their wives and
families and cattle into the village, and as the Church is the only
large building in the village with an iron roof, they propose
making this defence after the Dutch manner, by forming an

---

[1] The accepted modern spelling. The Reverend George Smith spelt the name Langabulela, and
there are many variants.

enclosure with their heavy wagons in front of the Church. While in the case of danger the women and children can take refuge inside the building, and should they be driven closely, they themselves can follow and defeat the old chief.

But although I think that danger attending those who join the expedition but slight, while I believe that the others might remain at their homesteads with proper safety, yet it is a time of anxiety for me. I have to do the best to allay the fears of those assembled near the Church. My congregation and people in St. John's Church, 20 miles off southwards, require my care. A great number of my parishioners are members of the Volunteer Force, and are upon the more or less hazardous journey forty miles northwards. Should the worst come to the worst I feel that my duty is to be in attendance upon their spiritual requirements,

I hope in my next report to be able to announce that Langalibalele's discretion has got the better of his valour and that temporary peace and spiritual progress are amongst the blessings which we may enjoy.

The Report for the quarter ending December 1874, after making apology for the long interval which had elapsed since he had last written, George Smith narrates the reasons.

The first is that during the past 12-14 months this period has been the scene of the Rebellion, and a sad scene too, and one which has left behind it disastrous effects.

In my report dated November 1873[1] I alluded to the panic which had seized the residents in the neighbourhood of the disturbance.

One of my Churches [St John's] was used by the Government for some months as a magazine, the other [St Matthew's] was looked upon as a rallying point and fortress for the inhabitants of the district.

Six Corps of Volunteers were ordered out and a detachment of the 75th Regiment and a company of the R.A. with two Armstrong guns came up to the scene of the outbreak.

On Sunday, November 2 [1873] I had a Parade Service for the Volunteer Corps previous to their departure upon active service. Immediately after the conclusion of the service, in accordance with the request of the Bishop of Maritzburg, I started off to

[1] March 1873.

meet the troops under the Drakensberg Mountains at a point 32 miles distant from this place.

I found several farmhouses deserted and the occupants of the one in which I passed the night were momentarily expecting an attack from the part of the Rebels for incendiary purposes prior to their intended flight.

We went through the form of retiring for the night, but an alarm at midnight (fortunately unfounded) so thoroughly aroused the whole household (consisting of ladies and children, one gentleman protector and myself) that we kept watch for the remainder of the dark hours and were not sorry when daylight came at last.

I had now to continue our journey towards the mountains and a very slowly one it was (excepting that I came across a few armed natives who declared themselves to be loyal). I arrived at the place of rendezvous just before His Excellency The Lieutenant-Governor, Sir Benjamin C. C. Pine, made his appearance.

The troops assembled were 137 men of the 75th Regiment and 35 men of the Royal Artillery. A small detachment of the Volunteer Corps had ascended the mountain to prevent the escape of the rebellious natives with their cattle, etc., by way of the passes.

The soldiers and the rest of the Volunteers were to close in upon the Insurgents who were believed to be in hiding beneath the mountain range.

I accompanied the troops the next day, or rather, I rode two hours before they started, to the site of their next proposed encampment, 16 miles northward. The wagons, with the tents and other necessaries, not arriving, we slept upon the grass with considerably less covering and more moonlight than was agreeable.

Early next morning a messenger arrived in haste with the tidings that a number of the rebels with Langalibalele at their head, taking with them thousands of their cattle, had escaped over the mountain and that five of our men, three Europeans and two natives, had been killed.

The troops were hastily ordered back to their last camp, and accompanied by two mounted and armed natives, who were the bearers of a despatch, I rode some twelve miles further northwards along the line to the spot where we expected to find the Volunteers encamped.

Our route lay through the Location occupied by Langalibalele's people, one passed through a great number of kraals, or native villages, apparently deserted except by a few stray dogs or fowls, and an occasional cripple or helpless old man or woman who had been deserted on account of their infirmity.

Through gardens of mealies [maize] , pumpkins, etc., unlimited pasturage and comfortable homes, all had been left because the foolish people did not know when they were well off, and because their old chief would hearken to the still more foolish young men instead of listening to those who were wiser as well as more advanced in years.

We reached the Volunteer encampment about mid-day. The men were under orders to march towards the mountains at daylight next morning. They heard (or thought that they had heard) firing in the direction of the mountain pass, but they knew nothing of what had taken place and, notwithstanding their anxiety, I did not think we ought to enlighten them upon that point, although I told the officer in command.

At half-past three in the morning the call of the bugle aroused us and preparations were made for the march. I should have liked very much to have gone with them, but I had other duties to perform, and St. John's Church, where my services were to be held on the following Sunday, was forty miles distant.

So I made my way to a small farm house, some ten miles off - in fact the only house within six and twenty miles; two bachelor sheep farmers occupied it, and as the rebels had stolen both their horses, they could not very well get away.

Whilst I was descending a veld near the place [Holmesdale] a thunderstorm came on and a terrific flash of lightning came into such close proximity to my companion and myself that we both fell straight to the ground, but we fortunately escaped serious injury.

This outlying household was the nearest to exactly opposite the Bushman's Pass. The front of the house commanded a view of the Insurgents' signal fires, and in the rear of the premises was a steep hill, the sides of which were full of caves covered with bushes, and the numerous fires betokened the presence of a large number of rebels. The house was very well barricaded inside, but having a thatched roof, it would hardly have stood a siege.

As armed native messengers were passing at all hours of the night and friends and foes are not easily distinguishable in the dark we had very little sleep during the two nights that I spent there.

On the Sunday week after the engagement at the top of the mountain, after holding Divine Service in St. Matthew's Church, Estcourt, I rode to the nearest Volunteer encampment, some 28 miles off and held evening service there.

At daylight next morning I proceeded across country to the

Military Headquarters, meeting on my way hundreds of native warriors, in full costume, chanting their war songs. My object was to obtain an interview with His Excellency the Lieutenant-Governor and get permission to accompany some expedition to recover our slain and give their remains the rite of Christian Burial.[1]

Sir Benjamin Pine was pleased to accept my offer. The expedition had been organized by Major Durnford[2] and within half an hour we started for the mountain.[3]

Our party, commanded by the Major, consisted of two Lieutenants and fifty men of the 75th, a Doctor, three Gentlemen Volunteers and myself; thirty Abasutos under their chief Hlubi, mounted and armed with rifles; thirty Zulus mounted and about 300 on foot, twenty pack horses, carrying ammunition, tents, provisions, etc., five oxen, thirty sheep and twenty goats.

The Bushman's River rises in the Pass which we had to ascend, and as our course - a fearfully rough one - lay up the valley of that river, we crossed the River twice and at night encamped in a deserted Kraal. At daylight next morning we marched on, crossed the river once more, and ascended a most tremendous hill, which, however, proved to be only a sample of many more that were in store for us.

The mountain torrents, too, were numerous, but the surrounding scenery was lovely. The Drakensberg Mountains formed a cloud-capped precipice on our right, whilst on our left, the rocky mountains that we had climbed and the rivers that we had crossed, looked like mounds of green velvet ornamented with silver threads.

At one o'clock in the afternoon we arrived at the foot of the Bushman's Pass, and although information had been given to the effect that Langalibalele was at the top with a strong band of his men to prevent those in charge of his cattle from being overwhelmed, we could see nothing of any opposing force. After camp had been pitched, and guard set, upon some rising ground commanding a view of the Pass, the Commanding Officer, taking with him all the natives, commenced the ascent of the Pass, and the orders were, in the event of heavy firing to follow at once

[1] An account of the action in which these fatalities occurred will be found in Appendix I.

[2] Major Anthony William Durnford, R.E., later killed at Isandhlwana.

[3] In *The Washing of the Spears* Donald R. Morris comments:'. . . the Reverend George Smith, minister of St John's Church in Weston. Something of a fire-eater, and a rabid High Churchman he had barricaded his church as a refuge for his parishioners and had ridden off with the Karkloof Troop.'

with the soldiers. We watched the whole party most anxiously. In about an hour and a half all had gained the summit of the mountain and then we listened for the firing which would be the signal for us to follow, but heard nothing. Suddenly, one solitary Kaffir could be seen descending the mountain with the speed of a wild goat, and with twenty men he arrived at our camp with a letter from the Major to the effect that some of the bodies were discovered, no rebels in sight; an officer, 25 men and I were to join the party at the top.

Lieutenant-Colonel A. W. Durnford, R.E.

Taking with us what possessions we could carry we started upon our upward course. The Pass is nearly two miles wide at the base and half a mile at the summit. The Bushman's River rises at the top and runs down a very rocky bed upon our right. The steep ascent is intersected by several smaller streams running into the larger one. The grassy slopes are all trodden down by the thousands of cattle which have passed over the mountain. The remains, however, of nearly a score which have fallen over the precipice are lying in the river. It takes us an hour and ten minutes to reach the top.

Just in front of us is a source of the Orange River which rises a few hundred yards from the head of the Pass and empties itself upon the west coast of our African continent.

The summit of the Drakensberg Mountains is roughly speaking the level of the country westward; there is no descent but a wild, bleak, undulating country.

In the stream to which I have referred the bodies of two of our volunteers and the two natives (a Zulu Christian Kaffir, Elijah Kambula, and Letsela Eduelfa, one of Hlubi's Abasuto tribe) had been cast by the rebels, after they had stripped and mutilated them. Half a mile lower down the valley we found the remains of the third Volunteer; his right hand had been cut off. He also was denuded of clothing.[1]

We passed a bitter cold night upon some huge ledges of rocks and morning came on with a cold drizzly rain. At five o'clock in the morning I accompanied the Major to select a spot where we might bury the slain. It was upon the very edge of the Pass, nearly 10,000 feet above the Indian Ocean (looking down upon the Colony of Natal, the Zulu country, the Transvaal and Orange Free State) that the graves were made and with rites of our Church and Military honours, the remains were interred of those who had fallen in the execution of their duty. A cairn of stone was made above their graves and by 9 a.m. we prepared to descend.

The rain which was falling rendered our descent both difficult and dangerous, but somehow or other between sliding and slipping and scrambling, in a very muddy and unpresentable appearance we arrived safely at the bottom eventually.

We had scarcely got down before camp was struck and orders were given to march back to Headquarters. This time we took a somewhat different route, but the principal difference was that

---

[1] From *The Washing of the Spears* we learn that the names of the three Volunteers were Bond, Potterill, and Robert Erskine, son of the Colonial Secretary. The Kaffir Kambula had been acting as Durnford's interpreter.

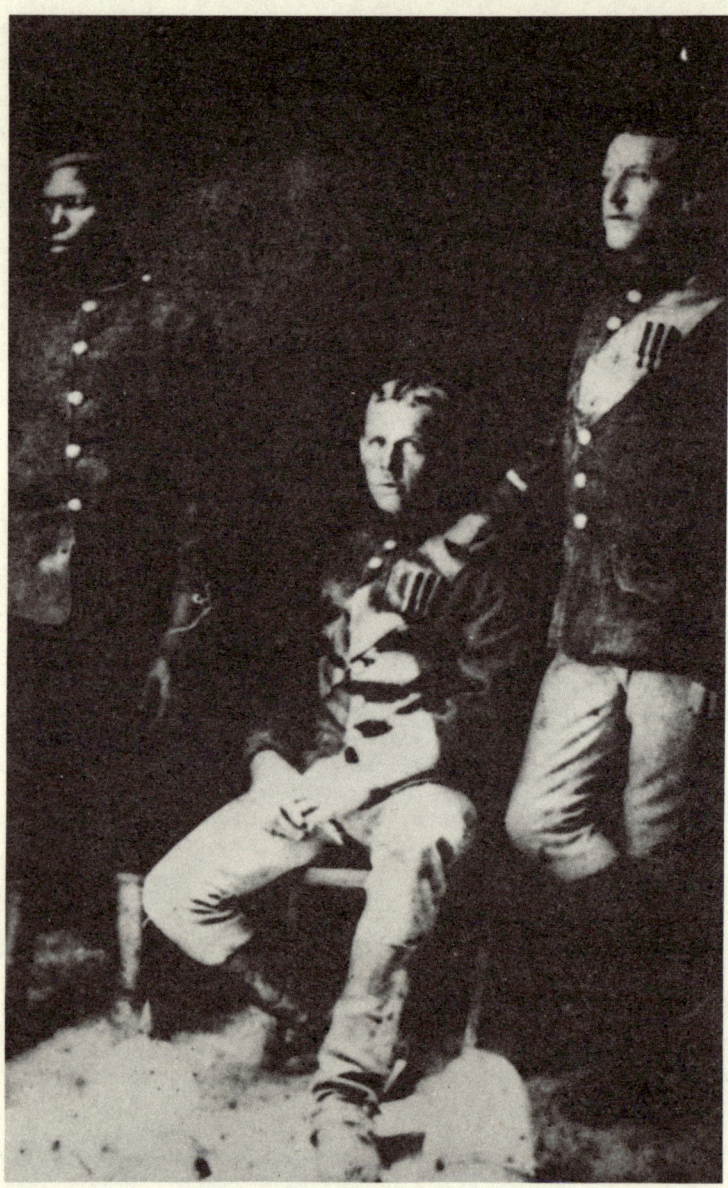

Three members of the Mounted Volunteers, 1873-81.

the hills we had to descend were much steeper than those we had previously climbed. I fastened my horse's bridle and allowed him to take his own course, while I walked. Sometimes he would slide or run on in front, sometimes follow behind.

At the foot of one frightful mountain, after we had crossed a river and halted to get our breath, messengers arrived from the camp informing us that the people of Hubli's tribe (which adjoined that of Langalibalele's northwards) were expected to make a rush for the same pass by which the others had escaped.

Orders were therefore given to retire to our last camp. One of the Lieutenants and I were desired to proceed to Headquarters. We had scarcely got a quarter of a mile before the rain came down in torrents. Three hours were those poor men and horses climbing that tremendous hill which we had just descended and we, too, with one native guide, had an equally hazardous and far journey before us. We journeyed on, but the rain increased and the mountain side became well nigh too slippery for man or horse; but we prosecuted our journey as best we could and arrived at the camp by 6 p.m., and right glad were all to hear of the success of our Mission. Sir Benjamin Pine thanked me in the kindest manner for accompanying the expedition and doing that which was only my duty.

I did not stay long in the camp but got on to Holmesdale and thence to St. John's Church for the Sunday service.

In my next Report [quarter ending March] I hope to be able to lay before you certain facts that will throw some light upon the late Rebellion of Langalibalele. The circumstances have been so misrepresented at Home (by Dr. Colenso and others) that I was anxious to avoid saying anything on the subject whilst public opinion (or rather passion) was so excited, fully assured that in calmer moments the truth would prevail.

In *The Washing of the Spears* there is a detailed description of the trial of Langalibalele, which the author considers was a disgraceful farce, of which he says that Theophilus Shepstone, wishing to avoid the tiresome formalities of trial in Roman-Dutch law, tried the case on Native Customary Law. A reviewer commented: 'It is only by the fiction of considering Sir B. Pine "a Native whose ignorance and habits unfit him for civilized life" that a crime against him is brought within Native Law at all.'

By the end of the second day of the trial Colenso had been able to procure the services of a lawyer to defend the Chief.

Although this received the assent of Sir Benjamin Pine, the Resident Magistrate refused to let him consult his client. The lawyer thereupon withdrew. Langalibalele, having been found guilty, was sentenced to life imprisonment on Robben Island. The whole of Natal acclaimed the sentence as a just one. The only voice against it was Bishop Colenso's. He was sixty years of age and worn down after twenty years of labour. He had lost many friends. Nevertheless he concentrated all his energies into a supreme effort to secure justice for the convicted chief and his tribesmen.[1]

In London it was suggested that a Royal Commission should be appointed. Sir Benjamin Pine dispatched Shepstone to put off an investigation. With him went Bishop Colenso whose arrival in London caused alarm in High Church circles, but he had not come to add more to theological controversies. He and Shepstone met the Earl of Carnarvon the newly appointed Secretary of State for the Colonies. He, too, felt that an injustice had been done to Langalibalele but above and beyond that he questioned whether the Colony of Natal was fit to manage its own affairs. Its autonomy, he decided, must be changed by making a confederacy of the different States in South Africa. To this end Sir Benjamin Pine would have to be replaced. Accordingly Major-General Sir Garnet J. Wolseley, G.C.M.G., K.C.B., was sent out to the Cape.

We now return to George Smith's promised Report for the quarter ending March 1875.

> In my last Quarterly Report I promised to refer to the question which has agitated the public mind, of the reality of the rebellion of Langalibalele and his tribe (who formerly resided in this district), and its results.
>
> I took no part in the political question involved, but as the Society's Missionary here, I feel bound, now that the excitement has well nigh subsided, to hand in the enclosed documents, which will give an insight into the real state of the case.
>
> I have given a copy of the address, presented to the Lieutenant-Governor by the inhabitants of this country, and you will find

---

[1] The following comment has been made: 'Probably these days far more South African churchmen would champion Chief Langalibalele's cause and side with Colenso.'

enumerated a score or more facts, patent to myself and every other resident here, perfectly conclusive as to the hostile intentions of these tribes.

You will find Sir Henry Barkly's reasons for declining to comply with the request of the Home Government to release Langalibalele, and the opinion of the Colonial Secretary of the Cape in the matter, and a still more important document from the pen of Mr. Brownlee, the Secretary for Native Affairs.

These documents will speak for themselves.

These papers published in *The Natal Government Gazette* of 6 April 1875, will be found in Appendix II. Doubly marked by George Smith, they prove that his opinions coincided with the people of the Colony rather than those of Bishop Colenso.

One other subject, however, I must be permitted to mention. I have several times spoken of Hlubi, the Chief of the Abasuto tribe. I saw a good deal of him during the various expeditions and this circumstance has resulted in one of the most promising openings for Mission work that I can possibly imagine.

Hlubi has been to see me several times to express his desire for a teacher to instruct him and his people. He is continually sending me urgent messages and has now promised to build a temporary house and schoolroom and pay something towards the salary of anyone whom I may be able to send him. His tribe is not a large one - about seventy men, wives, and a great many children; they live quite under the mountains, about 32 miles from here.

His people have nothing in common with the Zulus who live near them and are therefore much more likely to embrace Christianity, being unaffected by those strong influences which the Zulus always bring to bear upon each other. Hlubi is a young man and a most intelligent fellow. His people clothe themselves and live in square houses. They are occupied in agricultural and industrial pursuits and several of them possess wagons and oxen.

I need hardly say that the Bishop of Maritzburg is, with me, most anxious to undertake the work which seems open to us in such an extraordinary way.

I regret to state that the Government at present declines to assist me in my efforts to establish a Mission amongst Hlubi's Basuto tribe under the Drakensberg Mountains.

I made a Mission tour amongst the people, but unfortunately their chief was away from home at the time. I found them all very anxious to obtain instruction and they promised to send their children as soon as I could establish a school amongst them. They had already sent a large quantity of poles with which to erect a School house as soon as I could authorize them to do so. I have laid the matter before the Bishop and His Lordship is most anxious to commence the work amongst them at once.

I hope by the time my next report is due, that a suitable man may be found, but where the means for his support are to come from I do not know, but soon I feel assured they will.

A beautiful little Memorial Reredos by Messrs Cox & Sons has just been presented to my little Church of St. John the Evangelist, Mooi River, and the Church and Churchyard have been enclosed with a suitable stone wall.

I am sadly in want of a bell (a small one for St. John's, and a larger one for St. Matthew's).

Chapter Four

The Mission Progresses

In his report of Michaelmas 1875 the Reverend George Smith gives more cheering news.

Since my last report I am thankful to be able to chronicle much that has cheered me in my work. There are now three schools in the district. A private family school with 33 boys. A public day school at St. Matthew's school-church, Estcourt, ably conducted by James Henry Smith, who assists as Licensed Lay Reader. A public day school, 14 miles from Estcourt, at Blue Krantz River.

An interesting adult Baptism - a young girl, Hottentot parents, being in the service of a Scotch family 22 miles from Estcourt. On Sunday morning, August 29, special evening service, Master and Mistress answering for her as witnesses. Now bearing the name Emily Frances. Engaged to be married to a man of the same race called Piet, who has also placed himself under instruction with a view to Baptism.

Oct. 3 The Bishop of Maritzburg consecrated the new burial ground in Estcourt and held a Confirmation in St. Matthew's Church - 6 adult candidates.

On Sunday last the Bishop held another Confirmation in St. John's Church - ten candidates (nine adults). . . .

John Kismasale, native Zulu Lay Reader, night school assistant, serves several native villages and acts as my Interpreter.

Again his Report for the quarter ending 31 March 1876 gives news of the satisfactory progress of his mission. The question of a Mission to the Abasuto appears to have been satisfactorily resolved.

I am greatly encouraged in my work by signs of life, progress on every hand. The Church of St. John is improved by insertion of a neat little stained glass East window presented by members of the congregation. During the past six months congregations have been so large it may be necessary to provide greater accommodation.

The school-church of St. Matthew is well attended. There is a movement on foot to provide a new permanent church, leaving the present building for school purposes only.

I have received £18 for the purchase of a bell. Mr C. H. Dickens has presented the bell and handed over the £18 for the Building Fund.

St. Augustine's Mission to the Basuto Tribe is progressing favourably. The people are engaged in erecting a school-church of a primitive structure of ridge poles, sticks and clay.

There is an opening of work amongst the Zulus; 35,000 of them in the district.

A deputation of Idumas or Petty Chiefs came to see me about establishing a school and church mission. Some suggest they combine and furnish a school first in which the Mission could be started.

Chapter Five

Tragedy

The Reverend George Smith's Report for the quarter ending September 1876 contains a dramatic story of conversion.

Soon after Easter I baptized the first Zulu convert in this parish - Nagazi, who was 20 years of age. One night now a year ago he and several other companions were out in their Master's fields hunting porcupines. They were armed with assegais.[1] It was a bitterly cold night. A porcupine was seen and chased over a fence into a ditch beyond and then lost sight of. Presently in the dim light Nagazi shouted out that he saw it moving in the ditch, and rushing forward, stabbed again and again at the object when a fearful groan was uttered and he found that he had frightfully wounded - not a porcupine, but - an intimate friend of his own, the brother of one of his companions.

This unfortunate fellow (named Nell) had been away some fifteen miles to a Native beer drinking party and, returning after dark, thinly clad (if clad at all) having several small streams to wade through with the water at Freezing point, had become completely benumbed with the cold. This combined probably with the effects of his potations, induced him to take shelter from the biting wind in the ditch where he was aroused from stupor by the four of five thrusts of Nagazi's spear.

Nagazi and those who were with him were horror-struck when they realised what had been done. It was 3 o'clock in the morning. They at once aroused the Master and Mistress. The wounded man was conveyed to the house and it was found that he had been stabbed through the head and stomach and in the back and shoulder.

Surgical assistance was sent for and the Magistrate of the District acquainted with the facts. Nell, after a few days, showed signs of recovery. He exonerated Nagazi from all blame, and forgave him for his share in the unhappy transaction. Nagazi made Nell a present of the best cow that he possessed to show his regret.

[1] Zulu spears.

Then matters went on for some months. Nell's employers tended upon him most assiduously and supplied every want, and the unfortunate cause of the accident, ministered in every way to the relief of the sufferer. But, in deference to the superstitious notions of Nell's relatives, who watched him, he did not enter the sick man's room.

One day when he appeared to be getting better Nagazi passed near the door to ask after him. On that day he was taken worse.

'See', said his friends (?), 'the shadow of that fellow has caused this, and it proves that he intentionly worked this injury upon you. He is your murderer!!' Get an idea of this kind into a Zulu's head and nothing can alter his conviction. All the old women came wailing and howling and cursed their son's murderer.

All the young men and his fellow servants shunned his approach for 'had he not killed their brother?'

After lying for six weeks poor Nell died. The noise of howling and wailing (perfectly emotionless in the case of nine out of ten women performing it) was frightful, and the hate and revenge expressed by the men towards the unhappy cause of the death according to their own laws, if it were not for the White Man, would have soon ended in a second tragedy.

Poor Nell's grave, in accordance with Zulu custom (I don't know whether it is only locally or generally) was made after this fashion: His brothers selected one out of the way spot; a circular hole, some six feet deep, and three feet in diameter, was dug. Then an aperture excavation was made at the base. The body was then placed there in a sitting position, the sleeping mat of the deceased unrolled protected the entrance, against which were placed Knobkerries (knob sticks) and his other weapons. The ground was then replaced in the first hole, and one or two small stones unnoticeable to a passer-by mark the spot.

No sooner was Nell dead than his relations demanded recompense from Nagazi for the loss of their brother. Legally he was not bound to recognize this claim, but he generously gave them all the cattle he possessed; one cow to pay the Doctor's bill, and four others for the natives.

But in contrast to the malice, hatred and uncharitableness of those of his own colour and race, he was struck with the generosity and sympathy and unremitting kindness of his Master and Mistress to his fellow servants, and with tears in his eyes, he begged his neighbours to teach him something about that Spirit which prompted the Church to kindness and charity instead of hate and revenge.

After several months of careful preparation he was admitted into the fellowship of Christ's Church by Holy Baptism, in St. John's Church, Weston, Mooi River, in the Octave of Easter Day.

Although this was our summer here there was snow to be seen upon the Drakensberg Mountains. When returning from Church his Master asked him if he had noticed the Mountains and whether they reminded him of anything that he had heard? He replied in Zulu: 'Yes; "Thou shalt wash me and I shall be whiter than snow".'

He was baptized Stephen and takes the name of the village Weston as a surname.

Soon after he was baptized he heard that the girl to whom he was engaged to be married, had been ordered by her friends to give him up and become the wife of an old polygamist as her lover was a thoroughly bad fellow and had committed a foul murder. The girl would not believe this and desired to see him, but her father prevented her from doing so, and used such measures (as no one knows better than a Zulu) that without rendering himself liable to the arm of the law, he compelled the girl to forsake her intended husband and become the wife to a man who had paid the ten cows required for her.

When Stephen heard of this his first impulse was to go and undeceive her, so that in her estimation, at least, he might not be looked upon as a murderer, although she could never be his wife. But as he was gathering up his shield and weapons, better thoughts prevailed, for he saw the possibility of revengeful feelings taking possession of his mind when he should meet the man who had calumniated his character in order to obtain another wife and 'If he should be tempted to quarrel with the man might it not end in the sin with which he had already been charged?'

And to this day he is content to suffer the forfeiture of the good opinion of one whom he has esteemed most highly lest he may run into the temptation of endeavouring to clear himself from the foul stigma.

Stephen's conversion has so far influenced his family that his eldest brother Samuel has placed himself under instruction.

One of the numerous trials that a Zulu convert has to bear becomes even greater in Stephen's case, for he is very impetuous and high-spirited, and the least show of temper or hastiness calls forth the remark from some European: 'Yes, this comes of your being baptized. You are a nice sort of Christian Kafir, you are!'

He says: 'Nagazi will try to get the better of Stephen sometimes, but Stephen tries to stamp him out.'

This Report also mentions additions to his churches.

St. John's Church has just started with good open benches.

St. Matthew's now boasts of a fine stone font presented originally to St. Saviour's Cathedral, but as a very large font for St. Saviour's has lately arrived from England the original donor, who is now Lay Reader in this Parish, has transferred his gift to our little church.

Chapter Six

Christian Native Village

The concluding paragraphs of the Reverend George Smith's Report for the quarter ending 30 September 1876 embody an S.O.S. and a touching appeal regarding his salary.

> If the Society is able to continue my present income from the Natal Assistant Clergy Fund, I shall be able to keep my present sphere of labour; otherwise, rather than be referred to the 'Block Grant' which is already insufficient to support the numerous 'European work' Clergy which are dependent upon it, I would request that I am placed upon a footing with the Missionary Clergy, and either devote myself entirely to the Zulu native work, or if the Society wishes it, carry on that and the Basuto and other Native work, and perform my accustomed European ministrations in addition. But as the contributions from European sources do not compensate for the expense of Horses and the wear and tear of travelling some 150 miles weekly (and frequently a great deal more), such additional work undertaken is, one would suppose, hardly a sufficient reason for the reduction of a Missionary stipend.
>
> The Society will, I am sure, not misunderstand me or blame me for endeavouring to put one's local cares fairly before it, every detail of which I am able to substantiate.

We are not informed what steps the Society took in this matter of George Smith's stipend. There are no more reports from him to be found in the bound volumes of such documents in the archives of the S.P.G.

However, George Smith is mentioned in an interesting report of Canon J. B. Jenkinson, B.A., for the years 1876 and 1877.

At Estcourt the Reverend George Smith has bravely undertook

mission work besides the Mission to the Basutos under their Chief Hlubi.

His work, which is the foundation of a Native Christian Village is described in *The Net*[1] for January 1877.

In wishing the foundation God speed in the good work, I would warn him that the Natives who give sums of money towards the purchase of the 3,000 acres may claim to be part owners of the whole estate unless the part which they actually buy be distinctively marked off. But it would be better to sell a part than run the risk of their claiming a partnership in the whole. . . .

The establishment of the Christian Native Village is engaging Smith's attention. It comprises a farm of 3,000 acres with 44 Zulu huts and a population of 159. A Farm called Vigt Lager, or Fighting Camp, was the scene of a fearful whole day's fight between Boers and hordes of Zulus, lies 3½ miles from Estcourt. Farmers look coldly on the scheme as it draws away some of their trustworthy labourers. Several answer to come and live on the farm so that their children may be educated and brought up as Christians.

He hopes to transfer 12 acres to the Church for a Mission and to enclose part of this for a Burial Ground. He has been living five years amongst these people and until the last twelve months so nobly in the darkness of heathenism.

[1] *The Net* is the magazine of the Society for the Propagation of the Gospel in Foreign Parts, and on pages 86 and 87 of the issue of 1 January 1877, we find a letter from the Reverend George Smith from which we extract the following.

'Two little liberated Slave Boys from Manganja tribe of Shire River district, ages about 5 and 7, names Nawaya and Natgalolo. Their parents were shot and the children taken for slaves. Numbers of slaves were thrown overboard when a man of war was in pursuit of the dhow.

'Later - November 28 - they were baptized Edward and Robert in St. Matthew's Church, and took the name of Estcourt.'

Chapter Seven

The Zulu War

We must now leave George Smith toiling with zeal among his beloved Basutos and Zulus. Success for his efforts seemed imminent, and no doubt he was regarding the future with his usual optimism. However, the future was to channel that zeal in another direction. Already the horizon was clouded with the threat of another and greater war.

This came from the well-disciplined Zulu Army, which under its Chief Cetshwayo (Cetewayo) was considering the invasion of Natal. The first sign of such intention was the incident of two Zulu wives who had fled across the Tugela River in July 1878. They were dragged back by Zulu armed men, and were executed under the eyes of border guards. The Zulu Chief refused to hand over the culprits and he was sent an ultimatum by Sir Bartle Frere. One of the conditions of the demand was the demobilization of the Zulu Army.

Bishop Colenso hoped that the demands would be agreed to, but no reply was received from the Zulu Chief. After thirty days had elapsed the General Officer Commanding the Forces in South Africa, Sir Frederick Augustus Thesiger, commenced operations on 11 January 1879. Before that date he had become the second Lord Chelmsford, his father having died on 5 October 1878.

George Smith was caught up in the vortex of the Zulu War, for we find him taking up the appointment of Chaplain to the Volunteer Force. Thus on the outbreak of the war he was with the detachment consisting of B Company, 2nd Battalion of the 24th Regiment, commanded by Lieutenant Gonville Bromhead, left behind to garrison the Swedish Mission Station at Rorke's Drift.

Men of the Natal Native Contingent.

National Army Museum

His friend Hlubi, the young Basuto chief, whom he had fondly hoped would become a convert to the Christian faith, had been sought out by Colonel A. W. Durnford and was now in command of a large troop of Mounted Basuto Guides. They were skilled horsemen and, armed with Martini-Henry carbines, they proved excellent and dependable warriors. Their stirrups were of rawhide into which they thrust only their big toes. Later they were known as 'Durnford's Horse'.

Lord Chelmsford's force invaded Zululand early on the morning of 11 January. The first to cross the Tugela was a battalion of the Natal Native Contingent. These were followed by the 1st and 2nd Battalions of the 24th Regiment (2nd Warwickshire). On the 12th a small striking force was sent to seize the kraal of Sihayo. This was the Chief whose sons had killed the two Zulu wives who had fled across the Tugela in July 1878. In this action two Corporals of the Natal Native Contingent - Mayer and Schiess - were wounded. We shall meet them both in hospital at Rorke's Drift later.

On 20 January Lord Chelmsford's column reached a camp site at the foot of the conical hill of Isandhlwana, six and a half miles from Rorke's Drift. The following day he sent out a reconnoitring party under Major Dartnell, mostly comprised of members of the Natal Native Contingent. Dartnell sent back a message informing his chief that Zulus were to be seen in large numbers. Chelmsford, who wished to inflict upon them a sharp defeat, decided to support Dartnell with six companies of the 2nd/24th, his only squadron of mounted troops, and four seven-pounder guns under Colonel Harness. Moving off at daybreak on 22 January, he left the camp at Isandhlwana in the charge of Lieutenant-Colonel H. B. Pulleine, of the 1st/24th.

Pulleine was subsequently superseded by Lieutenant-Colonel A. W. Durnford, the latter being his senior by three years owing to his brevet rank. However, when Pulleine was about to hand over command to him, Durnford unwisely announced that he was leaving the camp to attack a body of Zulus, taking only two troops of Sikhali's Horse, followed by a company of the Natal Native Contingent. Pushing on into the valley beyond the high ground the mounted troops were faced with a Zulu regiment, some 4,000 strong, concealed in a ravine. They fell back in good order, but were unable to halt the enemy with their covering fire. They therefore sent a message by Captain George Shepstone, asking Colonel Pulleine for reinforcements. Durnford was now four miles from camp and ignored a warning from the vedette on Conical Hill that an immense impi was about to cut him off on his left from rejoining the camp.

At about 12.15 p.m. a staff officer named Captain Gardner, of the 14th Hussars, rode into camp with an order from Lord Chelmsford for Colonel Pulleine to strike camp and join his force at a new site. This coincided with the arrival of Captain Shepstone. In a hurried note Pulleine replied that he could not move as he had heard heavy firing on the left of his camp. To reinforce Durnford he sent the last troop of Sikhali's Horse. He then decided to extend his line from the spur to the north of the camp, the post of E Company of the 1st/24th under Lieutenant Cavaye. It was while he was trying to rescue Durnford, that that officer, finding himself outflanked, was making a rapid retreat to the camp. Pulleine's flank was now 'in the air' and he ordered a retirement by companies in succession. It was too late.

The two horns of the Zulu Army now encircled the panic-stricken camp. The transport drivers were striving to get over the Nek on to the road leading to Rorke's Drift. In their flight they were joined by the unreliable Natal Native Contingent, but there was no safety for them. The road was blocked by the right horn of the Zulus, which had gone round Isandhlwana Hill. The escape route to the south was likewise closed. The 24th, broken up into isolated groups, fought as long as their ammunition lasted, and then used their bayonets until they were overpowered. Captain Younghusband's company made a final stand on Isandhlwana Hill, and when they had used their last round, they charged downhill led by their commander. All were stabbed to death, except for one man who hid himself in a cave, and he was later shot in the head.

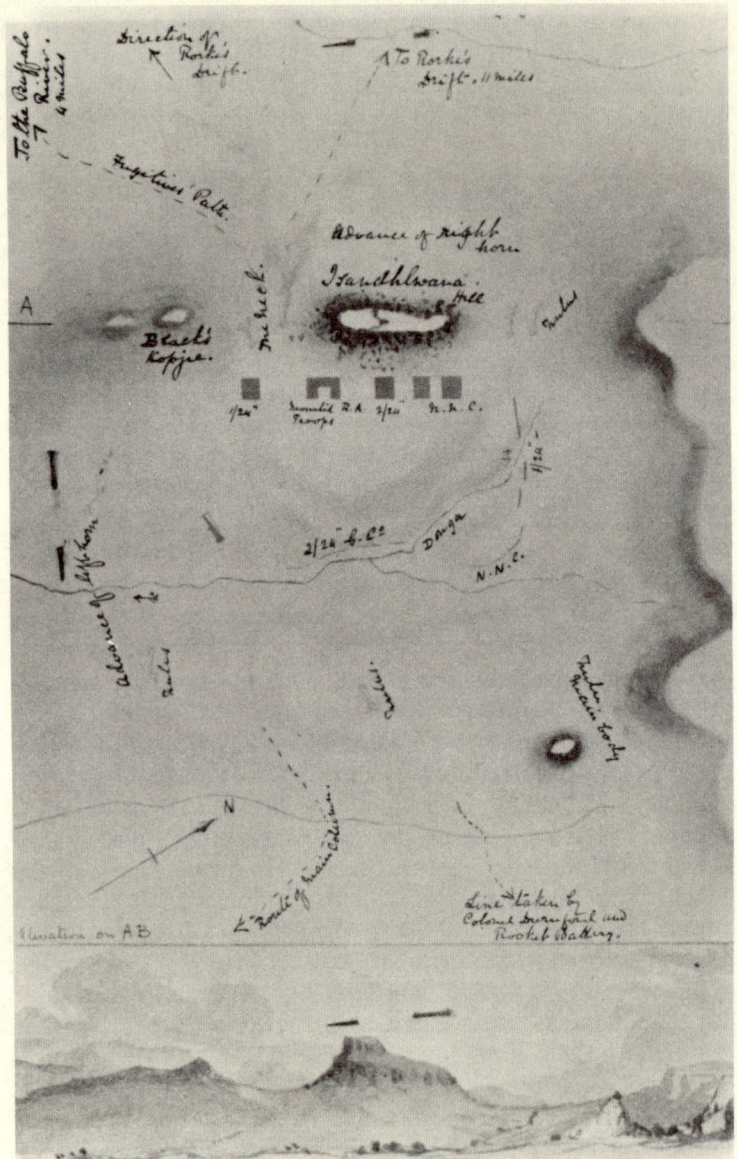

The battlefield at Isandhlwana.

Colonel Pulleine had ordered Lieutenant Teignmouth Melvill, the Adjutant, to ride off with the Queen's Colour. With him went Lieutenant Neville G. A. Coghill, who had injured his knee, and was also mounted. They reached the Buffalo River, where Melvill was swept from his horse by the current. He was helped by Lieutenant Higginson, Adjutant of the 2nd/3rd Natal Native Contingent, but both were swept down the river. Melvill was weighted down by his boots, empty scabbard, and the heavy staff of the Colour. Higginson now found it impossible to render further help. Coghill, who had succeeded in reaching the far bank, seeing the plight of the two officers, turned back to render assistance. As his horse entered the water it was shot in the head. This caused Coghill to fall into the river. He managed to reach the two officers and was able to drag Melvill to the shore but without the Colour which had gone downstream. Higginson, finding a horse, raced down with some men, but he was to late to effect a rescue. While fifty yards away he witnessed the end. Both Melvill and Coghill were overpowered by the Zulus after a gallant stand. Finding himself pursued Higginson rode off to safety.

By this time the two Colonels, Pulleine and Durnford, fighting to close to each other, had been killed. The Zulus plundered the empty tents, slaughtered the horses and cattle, and even the wounded men. There remained no survivors of either the 1st or 2nd Battalions of the 24th Regiment. Among those killed was Private William Griffiths who had been one of the five who had won the Victoria Cross in the rescue of officers and men of the Regiment from the Little Andaman Island in May 1867. Forty-three mounted men managed to escape before the tragic end and ten artillerymen survived. There were 1,329 corpses left on the stricken field. There was nothing now to stand against the invasion of Natal save the little garrison at Rorke's Drift under Lieutenants Chard and Bromhead.

Chapter Eight

Rorke's Drift

East of the Swedish Mission Station at Rorke's Drift was a commanding hill named the Oscarberg. Four men on its summit were watching to see if there were any Zulus about since distant firing to the east had been heard. These men were Surgeon-Major J. H. Reynolds, who was in charge of the military hospital, the Reverend George Smith, who had with him a telescope, and the Swedish missionary Otto Witt, and Private Wall. Witt had dispatched his wife and three young children a few days earlier to Pietermaritzburg, and he hoped to join them later in Durban. The three children were quite young. He had no seventeen-year-old daughter as depicted in the film *Zulu* neither did he himself stay to take part in the defence. We may consider the picture of him as a dipsomaniac unrealistic; but he certainly was no hero. In fact he reached Durban eventually and gave a very untruthful and garbled account of events to English newspapers. He was most unpopular in Zululand. Cetewayo had forbidden him entrance into his territory. With the colonists in Natal he was even more unpopular.

As soon as he saw some horsemen arrive Surgeon Reynolds descended the hill as he thought they might need medical aid. He arrived in time to meet Lieutenant Adendorff and Sergeant Vane of the Natal Native Contingent, the latter riding the horse belonging to Surgeon-Major Peter Shepherd, the Medical Officer on the field of Isandhlwana. This left Smith, Witt, and Wall on the Oscarberg. They had a clear view for some six miles of the Natal bank of the Buffalo River; but Fugitives' Drift, the scene of the last stand of Melvill and Coghill, was hidden from sight.

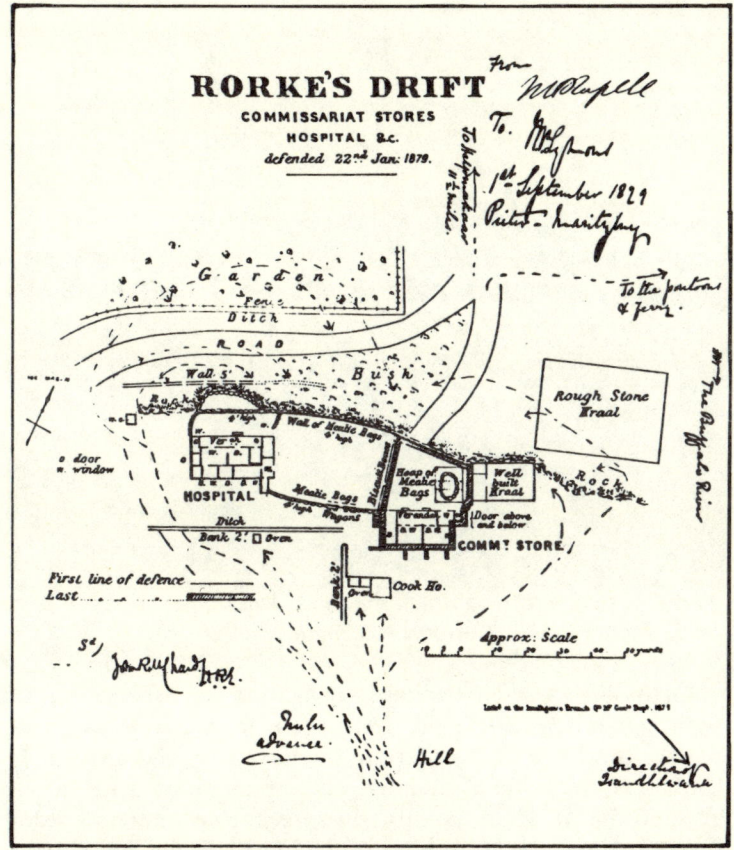

The plan of the Rorke's Drift defences from a drawing by Lieutenant J. R. M. Chard.

They were alarmed by the sudden appearance of a large force of Zulus near the distant bend of the river. It was the Undi Corps, comprising two regiments, some 3,500 strong.

George Smith immediately shut his telescope with a snap, and the three men came down the slope with all possible speed to give the camp warning. Harry Lugg, one of the defenders, remembered the shout they gave: 'Here they come, black as Hell, and thick as grass!'

The Eyebrow Hill from which the Zulu attack developed at 4 p.m. on 22 January 1879. The impi was about 4,000 strong.   Ian S. Uys

Otto Witt was an excitable man, and he became frantic with rage when he saw the destruction the garrison had made of his furniture and the ruin of his house and garden. In broken English he demanded an explanation. Then as he grasped the situation, he turned white, for nothing now stood between them and the huge Zulu impi. He did not stay an instant but, abandoning the homestead and station, fled to Helpmakaar to follow his family. As for George Smith he found no horse on which to make his escape. His Kaffir groom had ridden off with it. Perforce he was compelled to stay and thus become a national hero.

Here we may, I think, take up the Chaplain's own story of the Defence of Rorke's Drift as he recounted it in his Diary.

About three o'clock p.m., or shortly after, several mounted men arrived from Isandhlwana and reported the terrible disaster which had occurred.

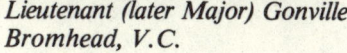

Lieutenant (later Major) Gonville Bromhead, V.C.

Lieutenant (later Colonel) J. R. M. Chard, V.C.

Lieutenant Bromhead, commanding the Company [B] of the 2nd/24th Regiment, at once struck his camp and sent down for Lieutenant Chard, R.E. (who was engaged with some half dozen men at the ponts on the river) to come up and direct the preparations for defence, as in the absence of Major Spalding the command of the post devolved upon him.

The windows and doors of the hospital were blocked up with mattresses, etc., and loopholes made through the walls both of the hospital and storehouse. A wall of mealies and other grain bags was made, enclosing the front of the hospital and running along the ledge of the rocky terrace to the stone wall of the kraal, which has been described as coming from the far end of the storehouse at right angles to the front of that building, down to the edge of these rocks.

A praiseworthy effort was made to remove the worst cases in hospital to a place of safety. Two wagons were brought up after some delay, and the patients were being brought out when it was feared that the Zulus were so close upon us that any attempt to take them away would only result in their falling into enemy hands.

So the two wagons were at once utilised to form part of the defensive wall connecting the right-hand front corner of the storehouse with the left-hand back corner of the hospital, also used as barricades underneath and upon the wagons. A barricade filling up the small space between the left front corner of the

storehouse and the stone wall of the kraal before referred to, and the blocking up of the gates of the kraal itself, made the outer defensive works complete. The men worked with a will and were much encouraged by the unremitting exertions of both the military officers, the Medical Officer and Assistant Commissary Dalton, all of whom not merely directed but engaged most energetically in the construction of the barricades.

The water cart, in the meantime, had been hastily filled and brought within the enclosure.

The pontmen Daniells and Sergeant Milne (3rd Buffs) offered to moor the ponts in the middle of the stream and defend them from their decks with a few men. But our defensive force was too small for any to be spared, and these men subsequently did good service within the fort.

About 4.30 p.m. the Zulus came in sight round the right hand end of the large hill in our rear. Only about twenty at first appeared advancing in open order. Their numbers were speedily augmented, and their line extended quite across the nek of land from hill to hill. A great number of dongas on their line of

British troops at Rorke's Drift. This photograph was taken the day before the battle and shows sandbags being erected on the rampart. Front row, left to right: possibly Lieutenant G. Bromhead, 2nd/24th Regiment; Surgeon-Major J. H. Reynolds; Assistant Commissary Dunne; Assistant Commissary J. L. Dalton; Colour-Sergeant Bourne, 2nd/24th Regiment; an unknown trooper of the Natal Mounted Police; Trooper Harry Lugg, Natal Mounted Police.

approach, a stream with steep banks, the garden with all its trees and surroundings, gave them great facilities for getting near to us unseen. The garden must have been occupied, for one unfortunate Contingent Corporal,[1] whose heart must have failed him when he saw the enemy and heard the firing, got over the parapet and tried to make his escape on foot, but a bullet from the garden struck him, and he fell dead within a hundred and fifty yards of our front wall.

An officer of the same corps, who had charge of the three hundred and fifty natives before referred to, was more fortunate; being mounted, he made good his escape and 'lives to fight another day'.

But the enemy are upon us now and are pouring over the right shoulder of the hill in a dense mass, and on they come, making straight for the connecting wall between the storehouse and the hospital, and then make a desperate attempt to scale the barricade in front of that building; but here, too, they are

[1] This was Anderson, of the Natal Native Contingent.

repulsed, and they disperse and find cover amongst the bushes and behind the stone wall below the terrace. The others have found shelter amongst numerous banks, ditches and bushes, and behind a square Kaffir house and large brick ovens, all at the rear of our storehouse. One of the mounted chiefs was shot by Private Dunbar (2nd/24th), who also killed eight of the enemy with as many consecutive shots as they came round a ledge of the hill. As fresh bodies of Zulus arrive, they take possession of the elevated ledge of rocks overlooking our buildings and barricades at the back, and all the caves and crevices are quickly filled, and from these the enemy pour down a continuous fire upon us.

A whisper passes around amongst the men: 'Poor old King Cole[1] is killed!' He was at the front wall: a bullet passed through his head, and then struck the next man upon the bridge of his nose, but the latter was not seriously hurt. Mr Dalton[2] who is a tall man, was continually going along the barricades, fearlessly exposing himself and cheering the men, and using his own rifle most effectively. A Zulu ran up near the barricade. Mr. Dalton called out: 'Pot that fellow' and himself aimed over the parapet at another, when his rifle dropped and he turned round, quite pale, and said that he had been shot. The doctor was by his side at once, and found that a bullet had passed quite through above the right shoulder. Unable any longer to use his rifle (although he did not cease to direct the fire of the men who were near him) he handed it to Mr. Byrne, who used it well.

Presently, Corporal C. Scammel [Scammell] (Natal Native Contingent), who was near Mr. Byrne, was shot through the shoulder and back. He crawled a short distance and handed the remainder of his cartridges to Lieutenant Chard, and then expressed the desire for a drink of water. Byrne at once fetched it, but whilst giving it to him, he was shot through the head and fell dead instantly.

The garden and the road - having the stone wall and thick belt of bush as a screen from the fire of our front defences - were now occupied by a large force of the enemy; they rushed up to the front barricade, and soon occupied one side, whilst we held the other; they seized hold of the bayonets of our men and in two instances succeeded in wresting them off the rifles, but the two bold perpetrators were instantly shot. One fellow fired at Corporal Schiess[3] of the Natal Native Contingent (a Swiss by birth and a hospital patient), the charge blowing his hat off. He

[1] Private Thomas Cole, 2nd/24th Regiment.

[2] Assistant Commissary James Langley Dalton was awarded the Victoria Cross - see Appendix III, page 86.

[3] For the chequered career of Corporal Schiess see Appendix III, page 90.

instantly jumped upon the parapet and bayoneted the man, regained his place, and shot another, and then, repeating his former exploit, climbed upon the sacks and bayoneted a third. A bullet struck him on the instep early in the fight, but he would not allow that his wound was sufficient reason for leaving his post, yet he has suffered most acutely from it since.

Our men at the front wall had the enemy hand-to-hand and were besides being fired upon very heavily from the sacks and caves above us in our rear. Five of our men were here shot dead in a very short space of time, so at 6 p.m. the order was given for them to retire to our entrenchment of biscuit boxes, from which such a heavy fire was sent along the front of the hospital that, although scores of Zulus jumped over the mealie bags to get into the building, nearly every man perished in that fatal leap: but they rushed to their death like demons, yelling out their war-cry of 'Usuto! Usuto!' Shortly after, they succeeded in setting the roof of the hospital on fire at its further end. As long as we held the front wall, the Zulus failed in their repeated attempts to get into the far-end room of the hospital, Lieutenant Bromhead having several times driven them back with a bayonet charge.

When we had retired to the entrenchment and the hospital had been set on fire, a terrible struggle awaited the brave fellows who were defending it from within. Private Joseph Williams[1] fired from a small window at the far end of the hospital. Next morning fourteen warriors were found dead beneath it, besides others along his line of fire. When their ammunition was expended, he and his companions kept the door with their bayonets, but an entrance was subsequently forced and, he, poor fellow was seized by the hands, dragged out and killed before the eyes of the others. His surviving companions were Private John Williams[2] and two patients. Whilst the Zulus were dragging out their late brave comrade, they succeeded in making a hole in the partition with an axe and got into another room, where they were joined by Private Henry Hooke [Hook],[3] and he and Williams—turn about, one keeping off the enemy, the other working—succeeded in cutting holes into the next adjoining rooms. One poor fellow (Jenkins), venturing through one of these was also seized and dragged away, but the others escaped through the window looking into the enclosure towards the storehouse and, running the gauntlet of the enemy's fire, most of them got safely within the retrenchment. Trooper Hunter (Natal Native Contingent) a very

[1] Had he survived Joseph Williams would undoubtedly have been awarded the Victoria Cross.

[2] Private John Williams (real name Fielding) was awarded the Victoria Cross - see Appendix III, page 93.

[3] Private Alfred Henry Hook was awarded the Victoria Cross - see Appendix III, page 87.

tall young man who was a patient in the hospital, was not so fortunate, but fell before he could reach the goal.

In another ward, Privates W. Jones and R. Jones[1] defended their post until six of the seven patients in it had been removed. The seventh was Sergeant Maxfield, who was ill with fever and delirious. Private R. Jones went back to try to carry him out, but the room was full of Zulus and the poor fellow was dead. The native of Umlunga's tribe, who had been shot through the thigh at Sihayo's kraal, was lying unable to move. He said that 'he was not afraid of the Zulus, but wanted a gun.' When the end room in which he lay was forced, Private Hooke (Hook) heard the Zulus talking with him; next day his charred remains were found amongst the ruins.

Corporal Mayer (Natal Native Contingent), who had been wounded under the knee with an assegai at Sihayo's kraal, Bombardier Lewis (R.A.), whose leg and thigh were much swollen from a wagon accident, and Trooper R. S. Green (N.M.P.), also a patient, all got out of the little end window within the enclosure. The window being high up, and the Zulus already within the room behind them, each man had a fall in escaping and then had to crawl (for none of them could walk) through the enemy's fire inside the entrenchment. Whilst doing this, Green was struck in the thigh with a spent bullet. Some escaped from the front of the hospital and ran round to the right to the retrenchment, but two or three were assegaied as they attempted it.

Whilst the hospital was being thus gallantly defended, Lieutenant Chard[2] and Assistant-Commissary Dalton[2], with two or three men, succeeded in converting the two large pyramids of sacks of mealies into an oblong and lofty redoubt, and, under heavy fire, blocking up the intervening space between the two with sacks from the top of each, leaving a hollow in the centre for the security of the wounded and giving another admirable and elevated line of fire all round. About this time, the men were obliged to fall back from the outer middle, and then to the inner wall of the kraal forming our left defence.

The Zulus do not appear to have thrown their assegais at all, using them solely for stabbing purposes.

Corporal Allen (Allan)   and Private Hitch[3] both behaved splendidly. They were badly wounded early in the morning but,

---

[1] Private William Jones and Private Robert Jones were both awarded the Victoria Cross - see Appendix III, page 88 and page 89.

[2] Lieutenant J. R. M. Chard was awarded the Victoria Cross - see Appendix III, page 84.

[3] Corporal William W. Allan and Private Frederick Hitch were both awarded the Victoria Cross - see Appendix III, page 85 and page 87.

incapacitated from firing themselves, never ceased going round and serving out ammunition from the reserve to the fighting men.

The light from the burning hospital was of the greatest service to our men, lighting up the scene for hundreds of yards around, but before 10 p.m. it had burned itself out. The rushes and heavy fire of the enemy did not slacken till past midnight, and from that time until daylight, a desultory fire was kept up by them from the banks and garden in front.

At last daylight dawned, and the enemy retired round the shoulder of the hill by which they had approached. Whilst some remained at their posts others of our men were sent out to patrol and returned with about one hundred rifles and guns and some four hundred assegais left by the enemy on the field; and round our walls, and especially in front of the hospital, the dead Zulus lay piled up in heaps. About three hundred and fifty were subsequently buried by us. They must have carried off nearly all the wounded with them.

Whilst all behaved so gallantly, it is hardly possible to notice other exceptional instances, although all their comrades bore testimony to such in the conduct of Colour-Sergeant Bourne (2nd/24th Regiment), Sergeant Williams (2nd/24th) and Privates M'Mahon (A.H.C.) and Roy (1st/24th).

It was certainly of the utmost strategical importance that this place should not be taken. Perhaps the safety of the remainder of the Column, and of this part of the Colony, depended on it.

In his book, *The Washing of the Spears*, Donald R. Morris makes the following comments of Padre Smith's actions during the defence of Rorke's Drift.

The Reverend George Smith, who had helped Durnford bury his dead in Bushman's River Pass, was a tall man with a great red beard. He had been appointed Chaplain to the Volunteers and was invariably clad in a tattered alpaca ecclesiastical frock[1] which had long since turned green with age. His general gullibility and unquenchable enthusiasm for military life afforded the other officers a measure of relief from the hardships of the field.

Chaplain Smith had slung a large haversack filled with loose cartridges about his neck. He circled the perimeter incessantly, filling out-thrust hands and expense pouches and replenishing his supply from time to time from the open boxes in front of the storehouse. He exhorted the men with wild Biblical phrases, sternly reproving every blasphemy and obscenity his ear caught.

[1] Cassock.

Chaplain Smith was still making his rounds, piling handfuls of cartridges beside the men at the embrasures and shouting his hoarse, homely encouragements.

On the fourth of February [1879] Major Wilsone Black led a small patrol out of Rorke's Drift to visit Fugitives' Drift. Scouts came across the bodies of Melvill and Coghill a half mile from the river, and the Reverend George Smith read a burial service over the grave dug in the shelter of the rock under which they had died. The patrol then descended to the banks, still littered with dead horses and men.[1]

It is commonly supposed that George Smith for his services at Rorke's Drift was offered the choice between a Victoria Cross and an Army Chaplaincy, and that he chose the latter. There is no evidence on paper to confirm this. Certainly no recommendation for the Victoria Cross was made, there being no papers concerning this at the Public Records Office.

[1] A fuller account of this ceremony and also of the burial of the remains of the victims of Isandhlwana is to be found in the reports of the missionaries, the Reverend Thornton Bulton and Canon Charles Johnson. These are filed in the archives of the U.S.P.G., 15 Tufton Street, Westminster. They form the subject of the next chapter.

The Reverend George Smith and Corporal Schiess, V.C. at Rorke's Drift - a detail of the painting by Alphonse de Neuville.

The Africana Museum, Johannesburg

Chapter Nine

After Isandhlwana

In a Report dated January 1879 the Reverend Thornton Bulton gives his view of the situation prevailing after Isandhlwana and his opinion of the Zulu. The Reverend Bulton was the Missionary at Clydesdale in the Diocese of St John's.

You know all South Africa has been disturbed for now more than a year by the Cape Frontier War. That happily is now over. Even at the distance of several hundred miles we felt its unsettling effects. In April last the tide of war was rather up to our very doors, but we were mercifully preserved from danger. Now again we have another war which will prove most serious and has already proved most disastrous. The Native mind seems to be determined to resist the advance of civilization and all that is right and good. The native chiefs feel that their power is leaving them so they are now doing all they can to resume it. As the native becomes civilized he cannot remain under the old unprogressive Chief and so as this is put down to the white man there is a determination to get rid of him if possible. After the present war - if it is prosecuted with vigour we shall have peace for many years. There is no doubt that the Zulus have long contemplated fighting with us and now we shall have a hard fight indeed. You will have heard of the terrible disaster that has already befallen our forces and the slaughter at Isandhlwana a week ago has brought trouble and sorrow and mourning to many a household in Natal and sadness to us all. From 50 to 60 of the best of Natal's sons have been cut off - over 500 soldiers of the 24th Regiment and others besides, making over 600 white men killed in one day. 20,000 Zulus attacked them, and when their ammunition was exhausted all were killed but five or six who escaped on horse-back. This small force had been left in charge of wagons, etc., whilst the main body went some miles off to look up the enemy. Before assistance could be rendered everything was lost. The Zulus spared none. The wagon drivers and leaders - many of them mere boys - were all killed. Then they stript the bodies of the slain and mutilated them in a most horrible manner. This severe loss will we hope teach our leaders a lesson of caution. It has taught us what the Zulus are - savage and barbarous more than usual with savage tribes. I sincerely trust that our country will not now rest until the Zulu power has been completely broken. Till this is done there will be no security and little progress in this part of South Africa. But you will have seen all this in the papers. I now refer to it to show that our work is still being hindered by the unsettled state of the country.

One of our new teachers who has just come begged leave to go home to look after the safety of his wife and family but the panic is over which has been caused by our severe reverses. Reports came in that upon us too natives in other parts near by us are again in agitation so that unless some decided advantage is soon gained in our land we may yet before long have the war at our doors. No doubt reinforcements have been sent for now. I hope they can come. What we dread more than anything is that the Zulus may get into some place where there are women and children and there will be none spared either death or mutilation. When the war is over I hope that we shall be able to show the Zulus that they think we try to destroy what is bad, yet we wish to teach them what is right and good. Our own natives tell us that we ought to treat the enemy in the way they treat us - kill every one and so teach them a lesson. They find it hard to understand why if we are the conquerors we take prisoners when Zulus do not do so.

The following is an extract taken from a Report of Canon Charles Johnson written at about the same time as the previous Report of the Reverend Bulton. Canon Johnson was the Missionary at St Augustine's, Isandhlwana, in the Diocese of Zululand.

On the 6th of October last, having learnt that Hlubi was appointed Chief over that portion of Zululand known as Setchwayo's district, I started from Springvale to ascertain if this move of his was likely to be the breaking up of St. Augustine's Mission, Estcourt (to which place I have been hoping to return when the new Incumbent for Springvale should arrive), or if his people would still remain at their old location, while himself with a few followers went to his new territory in Zululand. On arriving at Estcourt, however, I found that the entire tribe were leaving in a body for Zululand with their Chief. Hlubi himself was not there, having left some days previously, having been sent for by Mr. Frere, Resident Magistrate at Umsinga, to be shown the boundaries of his new district, but that hearing I was on my road up, he had sent back one of his men to see me and asked me to meet him [Hlubi] at Rorke's Drift, which is on the boundary between Natal and Zululand and then go on together to see his new location. Accordingly I drove on thither, and after a few days over a very bad road I arrived at Rorke's Drift and found Hlubi and a few of his men already there. I only stayed a day or two, long enough merely to take a slight glance round and to get an idea of what kind of country it was. I was very much pleased indeed to find that both Hlubi and his people were anxious that I should go with them. Hlubi said that he had been thinking that as the fatal field of Isandhlwana[1] was in the very heart of his district it would be very nice if a mission could be established there and on the very spot where so many brave men fell if a church could be built in memory of that sad disaster, in other words, a Mission church. I promised that I would do my best and if my Bishop would allow me I would go with them and continue the work amongst them which had been interrupted by the late war. On passing through Pietermaritzburg on my way back again I laid the whole matter before the Bishop of Maritzburg, telling him what I had done and what Hlubi and his people's wishes were. His Lordship took up the idea of a memorial church very warmly. He also thought that if possible I ought to go with Hlubi as he wished and that no time ought to be lost for it was a splendid chance for Mission work in Zululand and indeed the only opening at that time to the Church.

I revisited Springvale again on November the fifth, bringing with me the Rev. W. Greenstock, the new Incumbent, who most opportunely had just arrived from England.

Fully recognizing how good an undertaking it would be starting a new work so far away from civilization, it was not without my anxious misgivings that I sent word to Hlubi that I would accompany him and made all preparations for leaving Springvale. In the meantime the Bishop had written saying that he was going up to read the Burial Service at Isandhlwana and would be glad if I would accompany him, and thus make a definite commencement of the Mission, and as Mr. Greenstock's arrival enabled me to start at once I again left Springvale November 28th.

We were quite a party leaving Pietermaritzburg, consisting of His Lordship, the Ven. Archdeacon Usherwood, the Rev. G. Smith and myself, and our party grew larger as we went along,

[1]Canon Johnson uses the spelling 'Sandhlwana' throughout this Report.

Isandhlwana Hill, April 1879.

Mr. Fynn joining us at the Umsinga and the Civil Resident, Mr. Wheelwright, at Rorke's Drift. We reached Isandhlwana the day appointed throughout the Colony as a Thanksgiving Day for the restoration of peace. We rode over the Field and selected a good spot for the future Memorial Church on the site of the late camp of the 24th, and having erected a small iron Cross that we had brought up with us on a cairn of stones to mark the site, His Lordship read the Burial Service, assisted by the Ven. Archdeacon Usherwood, the Rev. G. Smith and myself, and the Celebration of the Holy Communion, after which he delivered a short address to the assembled natives (Basutos and Zulus). Mr. Fynn kindly acting as Interpreter, and then in a little more than a month after that Fatal Field and three months after the termination of the war, did meet in peace together by God's service they who had so lately been such deadly enemies, and who shall say what thought passed through the minds of friends and foes, Christian and Heathen, while entering that solemn and peaceful scene and contrasting it with that wild and horrible one, enacted but a few short months before us on that very spot.

It took us six days to get the wagon from Rorke's Drift to Isandhlwana, a distance of only twelve miles and usually accomplished in as many hours. The site that our little establishment occupies is excellently suitable. There is a fine spring of water which we have brought under the hill at some distance close to our doors in pipes made out of the iron ferrules of the tentpoles found on Isandhlwana battlefield (these lay thick on the ground where the tents had been burned). We collected them and fitted one into another and they make excellent water-pipes. We are well sheltered behind by a half circle of hills while in front some few hundred yards distance stands Isandhlwana itself. One of the first things we did after our arrival was to bring the numerous skeletons lying all about on the site of our future home. From what I can gather from the Zulus one or perhaps two companies of soldiers escaped, occupied this site as an outpost. There are two stone roads within a couple of hundred yards of each other and it seems that they were driven after a gallant defence out of the first kraal by the middle of the right horn of the Zulu army (it was composed of the Ngabeamathe Regiment) as it advanced. They then took up their position in the second kraal, which by all accounts they must have held well, but eventually their ammunition failed them, for they attempted a retreat on the camp but they were all killed before they had gone more than a hundred yards.[1] Of course I have only native evidence to go on and at best one can only conjecture and guess, but I think that there is little doubt that this is the place where the two companies of the 2nd/24th were supposed to be on picket duty and who were never heard of again fought and died.

---

[1] It is not easy to pinpoint which company this was, but it would appear to be likely that it was C Company of the 1st/24th, which was commanded by Captain Reginald Younghusband. His Company was on the extreme left of the line.'He got his bayonets fixed and pulled his men straight back, well clear of the slaughter on his right . . . . He retired across the back of the camp, forced up on the slopes of the mountain and rising along a rough ledge until he came to rest on a rocky platform at the southern end of the mountain, a hundred feet over the saddle. His men were almost out of ammunition, and had contested every foot of the way with bayonet and clubbed rifle. Sixty of them reached the platform, and they fought back to back in savage desperation until the last of them had been overwhelmed. A scant few, forced off the platform, died in the turmoil below.' (*The Washing of the Spears,* page 377.)

Chapter Ten

Ulundi

In his capacity as Chaplain, George Smith accompanied the force under General Lord Chelmsford in its advance upon Ulundi, Cetewayo's capital, and was present in the battle which took place on 4 July 1879.

There is an entry in the diary of Lieutenant G. L. Massy of the 94th Foot, dated 13 July 1879, which reads:

> 13 July. The first wash I have had since the 22nd June, it really seems incredible. To-day we had service and Parson Smith (the Rorke's Drift man) preached. He's a very good little [*sic*] fellow and used to be as keen on the fight on the way up as the best of us. Perhaps there was a grain of spite in this as all his farm and land have been destroyed by the Zulus. I hear some talk of giving him an Army Chaplaincy, and a better man they could not get. He seems to hit off all the motives and feelings of the men to a 'T' and, I should think, he would like the work. To-night we go on outpost, but as we are now allowed tents it is no great hardship.

Smith's incumbency of Estcourt was officially for the years 1872 to 1880, but he was Acting Chaplain for the period 1878-79. For his services he received the Zululand Medal with Clasp. Then on 1 January 1880 he was appointed Chaplain to the Forces in the Army Chaplains Department, as a reward for his gallantry in the Defence of Rorke's Drift.

From 1880 to 1881 he was Chaplain at Aldershot, and from 1881 to 1882 at Cork, and then in Egypt from 1882 to 1887. Here he again saw active service when he was present at Tel-el-Kebir. He was awarded the Queen's Medal for Egypt and the Khedive's Bronze Star in 1882.

The Reverend George Smith, C.F. and autograph.

Fighting in the Eastern Sudan broke out in 1884, and he was present at the Battle of El Teb on 29 February. Also during the Nile Expedition he was present at the action of Ginnis and received a Clasp.

On his return from Egypt he was Chaplain at the following stations: Shorncliffe, 1887-1890; Woolwich, 1890; Netley 1890-92; and Malta 1892-98.

Back again in England he had a four-year spell as Chaplain at Preston. Lancashire, from 1899 to 1903 (with a broken period at Caterham from 1900 to 1901). In the Garrison Church at Fulwood Barracks, his name is inscribed on the oak Roll of Chaplains (from 1848) given by the 4th Training Battalion (L. of C.) Royal Engineers on their departure from Preston in 1943.

From 1903 to 1904 there was a brief year of service at Harrismith in the Orange Free State, and then came his retirement in 1905.

A bachelor, he lived as Chaplain and also in retirement at Sumner's Hotel, Fulwood. With his patriarchal red beard, of which he was very fond, Daddy Smith was a familiar figure. There is in the hotel a picture of the Defence of Rorke's Drift, which is of special interest in that several of those who took part in it are named by George Smith himself.

In the Baptismal Register of the Garrison Church there are many entries signed by him. He conducted all services in a quiet manner and the atmosphere was that of a country church.

In a Regimental Journal there is a story told of how George Smith, on one occasion, said prayers in an officer's room at Fulwood Barracks in order to 'lay' a supposed ghost. The ghost was said to have appeared in the room and also on the staircase. There is still a swordmark on the wall where an officer is said to have struck at it one night. The story is not at all in accordance with his character, and one is inclined to think that the officer in question may have imbibed at mess too freely and had in consequence 'seen things'.

His death took place at Sumner's Hotel on 27 November 1918, at the age of seventy-three. The date on his tombstone in Preston Cemetery is inscribed 26 November, but two Preston newspapers state that the date was Wednesday, 27 November. His two elder brothers had predeceased him.

Grave of the Reverend George Smith, C.F. in Preston Cemetery.

J. Hodgson

Chapter Eleven

The Last Rites

The death of the Reverend George Smith took place on the morning of 27 November 1918, and the funeral with military honours was on 2 December. The service at the Garrison Church, Fulwood Barracks, was conducted by the Reverend W. Railton, C.F.

The coffin covered with the Union Jack was preceded by a firing party from the Depots of the North and East Lancashire Regiments under Captain Dawson. The escort was commanded by Captain Renham.

His niece, Miss Smith, was the principal mourner. Among those who followed were Messrs J. Seaman of London, J. Booth, J. Forshaw, J. Whittaker (Snow Hill), H. Waterhouse (representing A. A. Gatti and Company), and E. Herling.

A number of officers from Fulwood Barracks attended at the cemetery, including Colonel Costobodie, Colonel Daniels, D.S.O., Colonel Wild, Major Goddard, Major Daubery, Major Williamson, and Lieutenant Greenwood.

Included among the wreaths was one from the officers of the 24th Regiment (South Wales Borderers): 'In Memory of Rorke's Drift'.

The inscription on the gravestone reads:

TO LIVE IN THE HEARTS WE LEAVE BEHIND IS NOT TO DIE
SACRED TO THE MEMORY OF THE
REV. GEORGE SMITH
CHAPLAIN TO THE FORCES
ONE OF THE HEROES OF RORKE'S DRIFT
WHO DIED NOV. 26th 1918
AGED 73 YEARS
HE WAS A BRAVE AND MODEST
CHRISTIAN GENTLEMAN

Langalibalele's Rebellion

For the following résumé of the events preceding the visit of
the Reverend George Smith to the scene of the battle at the
Bushman's River Pass I am greatly indebted to Donald R.
Morris's narration in *The Washing of the Spears*.

Langalibalele was the Hereditary Chieftain of the amaHlubi, who
were Zulu refugees kin to the Basutos. The Government was
concerned that they were acquiring firearms. Young men of the
tribe had been slipping away to the diamond-fields where the
miners offered a gun in place of a season's wages. These firearms
were not registered when the men returned to Natal, otherwise
they would have been confiscated. Langalibalele was a
dissolute old ruffian. He sympathized with his tribesmen and
adopted a typically native solution - he temporized. He first
pleaded ignorance and then ill-health. He ignored orders to report
in person. To Theophilus Shepstone such conduct was
tantamount to rebellion, and he promised to fetch Langalibalele
in person. The Chief persuaded the neighbouring amaPutini to
hide some of his cattle in caves in the Drakensberg Mountains. He
then made for the high veld with his warriors and the rest of the
cattle. Shepstone regarded this flight as treason, but Langalibalele
was hardly a British subject in the accepted sense of the word. No
law denied him the right to leave if he chose. Nevertheless, if he
got out of Natal with 10,000 men his act of defiance might
destroy the shaky control exercised over the other hereditary
chieftains.

An expedition was sent under the command of Lieutenant-
Colonel Thomas Milles of the 75th Regiment. It consisted of two
companies of the 75th, and some Colonial Volunteers, and 8,000
Natal Kaffir levies commanded by Zulu-speaking colonists. Major
Anthony William Durnford, R.E., was appointed Chief of Staff.
The plan devised by Milles was to move a force up the high veld
to near the Bushman's River Pass. From here it was to drive
Langalibalele into the arms of the troops waiting below. A light

force under Major Durnford left on 2 November 1876. But very little was known about the passes and in the event the Kaffirs never reached the top.

Durnford had under him a young inDuna, named Hlubi, and a mission native, Elijah Kambula [mentioned by George Smith] as interpreter. The Europeans comprised the Richmond Mounted Rifles and the Karkloof Troop of the Natal Carabiniers, of which Captain Charles Barter was the senior officer and Sergeant Clarke, who had had long service in the Regular Army, was the senior N.C.O.

Setting out at dusk, Durnford's careful orders to Barter were upset. The packhorses, laden with rations and ammunition, wandered off and were lost. Neither the packhorses nor the searchers sent out to scout for them turned up until all was over. The steep trail to Giant's Castle Pass led the column along narrow ledges and among tumbled rocks. A number of exhausted men fell out. Then Durnford's horse slipped and he was dragged backwards over a cliff. He was badly injured - with a severely cut head, a dislocated shoulder, and two broken ribs. However, he had himself bound up and soldiered on. In the Pass Durnford, delirious with pain and exhaustion, called a halt. In the bitter cold, before dozing off, he dictated and signed orders sending a few baTlokwa on ahead to get to the top of Bushman's River Pass at the time agreed upon.

He woke before midnight and in the light of the rising moon pressed on with his command. By now his injuries had worsened and he was unable to stand and so he was carried. The top was reached at 4 a.m. One of the natives reported that all was well at Bushman's River Pass, twelve miles distant.

At the Pass they found some cattle and about a hundred herders, most of them armed. More cattle and herders could be seen below. Durnford's men had not eaten since dawn of the preceding day. He, therefore, gave permission for them to catch and slaughter a beast. When he offered to pay for the beast, Barter told him that Natal Kaffirs always fed Government troops free of charge. This did not lessen the obvious hostility of the herders, and the amaHlubi in the Pass would not permit the herd to descend. Durnford rode out with Elijah Kambula and gathered the herders together. He read Sir Benjamin Pine's proclamation and told the herders to inform their fellows that no harm would come to them if they returned to their location. More herders came to join those in the Pass and these Durnford ordered back. A spokesman replied that they would only descend if Durnford and his force preceded them as they feared an attack. When Durnford refused the request he was threatened. He would have been killed but for an inDuna named Mabuhle who arrived and struck the men who had shaken their assegais or pointed their guns at Durnford. Mabuhle begged him to leave before his men got out of hand.

With the amaHlubi taking cover Durnford sent for help and reinforcements. He moved into a stronger defensive position, deploying Volunteers to cover him. Then Barter rode back to inform Durnford that the Carabiniers could not be relied upon and that a retreat was advisable. Sergeant Clarke also lost his head. He rode among his men saying they were surrounded and would all be massacred! The men, on the verge of breaking, were confronted by Durnford and Kambula, who attempted to move the amaHlubi. When Durnford called for men to stand by him only three responded. Two of them, Bond and Potterill, offered to ride down to the amaHlubi and show there was no cause for alarm. The third man was Robert Erskine, son of the Colonial Secretary. He had tended Durnford the preceding night. The Volunteers turned, and as Clarke shouted 'Form fours!' there was a shot from the amaHlubi, and this was followed by a volley which killed Bond and Potterill. Erskine's horse reared, the saddle slipped, and he fell and was assegaied. The Karkloof Troop broke and ran. Elijah Kamubula's horse was cut down and he was shot dead. Durnford himself was stabbed twice. With his right hand he drew his revolver and shooting down two of his assailants he managed to ride to safety.

Hlubi rallied his baTlokwa, but the amaHlubi followed them the twelve miles to Giant's Castle Pass. Here Durnford found Lieutenant Parkinson with twelve stragglers. With rage and frustration he berated his errant command and held up to them the example of the baTlokwa members of which caught his bridle as, alone, he turned back to calm the bolting Volunteers. They led him down the Pass and he reached the main camp after midnight. Despite his many severe wounds he never faltered and for the rest of his life he lacked the use of his hand and forearm - a handicap in the later fighting at Isandhlwana.

It had been a bitter and disastrous defeat for Durnford on his first active command. Langalibalele had got clean away and if the 30,000 Natal Kaffirs followed the lead of the amaHlubi then the Colony itself was in serious danger. An unpopular man, Durnford was severely blamed for the débâcle and his unpopularity increased. The defeat was made still more unpalatable by the official report he made on the appalling behaviour of the Volunteers - and this they deserved. From his indictment Durnford exonerated Bond, Potterill, and Erskine, the three courageous Volunteers and the interpreter Kambula with his companion Letsela Eduelfa, together with the baTlokwa.

Durnford himself had his defenders - notably Dr Colenso and Sanderson, the Editor of *The Natal Colonist*.

Unaware of the feeling against him, Durnford rode into Pietermaritzburg two days after his descent from the mountains. Here he organized a force of Regular troops and returned to Bushman's River Pass. It was this expedition that the Reverend George Smith joined. In *The Washing of the Spears* it is recorded: 'Durnford buried his five companions, and he also buried and erected a cairn over the two amaHlubi he had shot. The service was conducted by the Reverend George Smith, minister of St John's Church in Weston.'

Colenso had followed the campaign in the newspapers supplemented by private correspondence. He considered Langalibalele guilty, but was opposed to any sort of trial. Letters from colonists were published in the newspapers, complaining of atrocities - rebels had been shot and stabbed by native levies after they had surrendered. On this matter Colenso questioned Durnford closely and obtained an admission that such incidents had indeed occurred. When Shepstone returned to Pietermaritzburg, Dr Colenso took him to task about the atrocities. Every act was defended by Shepstone. Thus was revealed the difference between the Bishop's concern for the Africans and Shepstone's contempt for them. The break between the two men was sudden, complete, and permanent.

Langalibalele wandered about the veld for six weeks and was then betrayed. Taken in chains to Pietermaritzburg, he was tried in January 1874 on charges of murder, treason, and rebellion.

The trial is described in *The Washing of the Spears* as a disgraceful farce. The case was tried under Native Customary Law and Sir Benjamin Pine sat as Supreme Judge. He was assisted by Shepstone, four European magistrates, and six appointed native chieftains. Langalibalele was not represented by counsel, Colenso having failed to find a man willing to defend him.

The Natal Government Gazette, 6 April 1875

FURTHER PAPERS RELATING TO THE KAFIR OUTBREAK IN NATAL

(In Continuation of C. 1121 of 1875)

No. 1

Governor Sir H. Barkly, K.C.B., G.C.M.G., to the Earl of Carnarvon.
— *(Received February 1.)*

Government House, Capetown,
January 5, 1875.

My Lord.—Your Lordship's despatch of the 4th ultimo,* informing me of the decision of Her Majesty's Government on the case of Langalibalele, reached me on the 31st ultimo, and I lost not a moment in bringing it under the consideration of my Responsible Advisers, with a view to obtaining the promise of their co-operation in making arrangements for the location of the Chief and his son, after their liberation from Robben Island, on the mainland of this Colony.

2. I regret to have to state that, for the reasons assigned in the enclosed Minute, Mr. Molteno and his colleagues, after much deliberation, conducted with every disposition to act in accordance with the opinions of Her Majesty's Government, feel themselves precluded from taking steps towards giving effect to your Lordship's wishes.

3. I regret this, not only on account of the inconvenience that may thus be occasioned to Her Majesty's Government, but for the sake of the colony itself; because, whilst still adhering to the opinion I felt it my duty to express to your Lordship five months ago,† that it was better for the peace of South Africa, as well as their own security and comfort, that Langalibalele and Mahlumbuli should remain on Robben Island for some time to come, I cannot but perceive that if their release thence is determined on, it will be far safer for all interested in preventing Kafir wars to keep them, as Your Lordship proposes, under strict surveillance somewhere in the neighbourhood of Cape Town, than either to send them back to be confined under stringent restrictions in Natal, or pardon them on conditions only of their not returning to that Colony.

4. That there would be some risk in the first case, as pointed out by Mr. Brownlee in a Memorandum (which, together with the note from Mr. Molteno on the subject, forwarded privately last mail, are attached to the Minute), of their escaping into the Trans-kei, where so many of their relatives live, and causing, either intentionally, or from the superstitious reverence with which Langalibalele is far and wide regarded, serious disturbances, cannot be denied; but there would be still more danger in their return to Natal; and it would assuredly be

the most dangerous course of all to permit them to proceed triumphantly direct from Robben Island to the very flanks of the Drakensberg, as they would do in the last case.

5. I fear, however, that the conclusions to which my advisers have come, will prove to be in closer accordance with the views entertained by the vast majority of the colonists of European descent, than those I have above expressed, and that it would have been vain, consequently, to have attempted to withstand the agitation which will arise whenever the despatches are published.

6. Under these circumstances, I see no alternative but to await your Lordship's instructions in the matter before moving further, detaining Langalibalele and his son on Robben Island until either a formal pardon from the Queen is forwarded in their favour, the disallowance of Act No. 3 by her Majesty is announced to me, or the Natal Government apply to this Government for their re-delivery.

7. Meanwhile steps will be immediately taken to ameliorate the condition of the prisoners there by allowing them all possible indulgence, and putting them as nearly as possible on the same footing as if they had been transferred to a location of their own on the mainland, where it would have been necessary, indeed, to keep them under much stricter regulations than are prescribed in their present insular home.

8. Robben (*i.e.*, Seal) Island is not, as seems to be supposed by the British public, a penal establishment, and has not been so for years, except in so far as it has been used as a secure place of custody for rebel Kafir Chiefs, and as the lunatic and benelovent asylums upon it occupy but a comparatively small portion of its area, there is nothing to prevent Langalibalele and Mahlumbuli from occupying their own kraal, keeping their own cows, cultivating corn, and living, if they can induce any of their wives or other members of their tribe to join them, exactly in the same position as they are used to.

9. None of the former, I believe, volunteered to accompany the prisoners when they embarked at Natal, but perhaps Mr. Shepstone may be able now to persuade one or more to come down by an early steamer or possibly, failing this, some of the Zulus or Fingoes now engaged on the railways in this part of the Colony may be hired to attend on the old Chief.

10. Trusting that these arrangements will meet with your Lordships approval, as the best that could, under all the circumstances, be made.

I have &c.

(Signed) HENRY BARKLY.

* [Vide No. 30 of previous Paper C. 1121 of 1875.]
† [Vide despatch of August 14, 1874, No. 10 of same Paper.]

Inclosure 1 in No. 1.
*Minute of a Despatch from the
Right Hon. the Secretary of State
for the Colonies to his Excellency
Sir H. Barkly, K.C.B., G.C.M.G.,
dated December, 4, 1874.*

Ministers having carefully considered this despatch, as also that addressed to Lieutenant-Governor Pine, on the subject of Langalibalele and his son, now confined on Robben Island. together with your Excellency's Minute expressing confidence that Ministers would authorize you to inform Lord Carnarvon, by return of post, that they are prepared to do all in their power to carry out the wishes of the Imperial Government, cannot do otherwise than express their very great regret that the Imperial Government should have adopted a course of action which, it is feared, will prove to be most detrimental to the peace and security of this Colony, and of South Africa generally.

Mr. Molteno's note to your Excellency, which it was deemed advisable to transmit to Lord Carnarvon by last mail, as also a Memorandum drawn up by the Secretary for Native Affairs, which accompanies this Minute, give fuller expression to the views of the Ministers on this subject.

While it will at all times be the earnest desire of the Ministers to co-operate with the Imperial Government, occasions may arise when it would be impossible to do so without sacrificing the interests of the Colony.

Such an occasion seems now unfortunately to have arisen.

This Government cannot give its assent to Langalibalele and his son being "removed from Robben Island to a location to be set apart for him within the Cape Colony, under strong restrictions against re-entering Natal."

The laws of this Colony give the Government no such power as would be necessary for enforcing such restrictions, and it is hoped that upon the Imperial Government being made aware of the want of the necessary power to confine these men to any particular location or district, if once set at liberty, it will see the reasonableness of the objections to having them let loose in the Colony to become a certain source of danger and trouble.

Nor can Ministers avoid noticing that the Imperial Government, whilst exercising clemency to this Chief and his son, by assigning to them a location within the Cape Colony, has given the Colony no opportunity of expressing any opinion as to how far its interests and rights would thereby be compromised or affected.

The Imperial Government has determined to disallow Act No. 3 of 1874; this done, the action taken by this Colony in this unpleasant business will be virtually set aside, and there would appear to be no alternative, in so far as Ministers are concerned, but to revert to the position they were in before the Act was passed, by returning Langalibalele and his son to Natal.

But as this would be in opposition to the desire of the Imperial Government, Ministers will be glad to learn in what other way this Government may be relieved of the charge as soon as Act No. 3 of 1874 ceases to be law.

(Signed)   J. C. MOLTENO.

Inclosure 2 in No. 1

Colonial Secretary's Office,
Capetown, December 24, 1874.

To His Excellency Sir H. Barkly,
K.C.B., G.C.M.G., &c., &c.

My dear Sir,

Judging by the articles and correspondence in the "Times" and other English newspapers lately received, it seems clear that Bishop Colenso has carried out his intention of agitating on the Langalibalele matter, and is endeavouring to create an impression that he has been cruelly and unjustly punished. In the absence of anything which would indicate the view Her Majesty's Government would be likely to take, I confess to some anxiety lest they may be induced to yield to pressure in the direction of releasing the two prisoners now on Robben Island, the effect of which, on the peace and security of this Colony, might be most disastrous.

Whatever exception may be taken to the proceedings of the Natal Government throughout this unfortunate business, certain prominent features must not be lost sight of.

It is unquestionable that Langalibalele deliberately intended to and did defy the Government, and that, had he not been made prisoner quickly the probability—indeed, almost certainty—is that very serious disturbances would have taken place amongst the native tribes within and immediately beyond this Colony, to say nothing of Natal, which, if once commenced, there is no telling where they would have ended, and what would have been the ultimate consequences.

Secondly, that with all native tribes the one opinion and idea is that this Chief has defied the Government, has been checkmated and defeated in his purpose, and is now justly undergoing punishment; indeed, that he has been leniently dealt with.

Should he now be released, the idea with these people will be that it is from fear and distrust on our part as to the success of our policy; consequently our difficulties in the management of the natives would be increased enormously, so much so that it would be impossible for us to preserve peace and the satisfactory state of affairs which have now existed for the last twenty years and upwards, in which case the question would necessarily arise as to whether the Home Government could leave us to ourselves to bear the brunt of a policy essentially their own.

But this is not all, for while it is quite possible that British power, which has spent so many millions and sacrificed so many lives in an Abyssinian expedition, and lately on the west coast of Africa, may say, no matter at what cost, we are determined to enforce our views of what we consider abstract justice in this case of Langalibalele, what would be the position of the colonists and white inhabitants of the whole of South Africa? To them it would be a question of life and death; their property would be sacrificed and their lives imperilled to a fearful extent should anything like a war of races be now brought about.

Every year that now passes strengthens our position and renders any serious disturbance of our relations with the native tribes less and less likely; but should a war be now brought about it would certainly not be a small one, and, no matter what the result, could not do otherwise than throw back civilization in South Africa for an indefinite period.

If it were possible to get all these circumstances properly considered and weighed by British statesmen, I feel sure that they would hesitate to take steps which would certainly tend to bring about such a state of things, simply because to the nicely-balanced judicial minds of a few enthusiasts the proper forms of trial have not been adhered to, and perhaps more severe measures in regard to the mass of the people of the rebellious Chief have been resorted to than was warranted, but which latter has since been redressed as far as possible.

Under any circumstances, I feel it is necessary that Her Majesty's Government should be fully informed as to the consequences likely, in the opinion of those supposed to be in a position to judge, although not responsible for what has been done in Natal, to ensue.

It will be for your Excellency to judge in how far it will be advisable to inform Her Majesty's Government of the view taken in this matter before any definite action is perhaps taken.

I remain, &c.,
(Signed)   J. C. MOLTENO.

Inclosure 3 in No. 1
Memorandum
In re Langalibalele.

If the Act No. 3 of 1874 were repealed, and Langalibalele were located on the main land, this Colony would possess no power to exercise any control over him; he would therefore very soon find his way overland to the borders of Natal; for an appeal to the members of his tribe at Natal, or even to his countrymen and connections in this Colony, would at once place at his disposal abundant means for that purpose.

In considering the effect on the Native tribes of the release of Langalibalele, it cannot be overlooked that he possesses even greater influence, from his reputed powers as a magician, than he does as a Chief of a large and powerful tribe.

Last year, when I visited the Transkei, heavy floods had fallen; these were attributed to Langalibalele's captivity, and it was said that until he was liberated the land would be inundated by floods, which would be attended by loss of life, destruction of stock, and devastation of crops. The unprecedented floods of last month, extending from Natal to the eastern divisions of this Colony, sweeping away our bridges and causing enormous damage to property of all kinds, will, in the minds of the natives, greatly enhance the importance of Langalibalele, and will tend to confirm the predictions of last year.

Langalibalele's influence, both as magician and Chief is greatly strengthened by his extensive family connections with almost every tribe between the Colony and Natal; his own children, apart from other relatives, amounting to the number of 54 sons and 68 daughters, many of whom are influentially married amongst these various tribes.

All the natives feel, and those friendly to us admit, that Langalibalele has received substantial justice. His release would be considered as a sign of weakness rather than an act of clemency on the part of the British Government, and would be attributed to his power as a magician. His importance would thus be magnified in the eyes of all the native tribes both in the Colony and Natal. Their minds would become unsettled and our influence impaired.

Macomo, the greatest general known to the natives, who took and held possession of a portion of the Colony for three years, in spite of all attempts to eject him, until expelled by our united efforts under Sir G. Cathcart, died recently on Robben Island, after a long exile.

Umhlala, the most crafty and politic of Kafir Chiefs together with other influential Chiefs transported to Robben Island for offences committed by them, were pardoned, and only after a lengthened captivity.

Lydx, the celebrated prophet, under whose inspiration in 1819 the Gaikas were conquered with great slaughter by the Hlambis and driven out of their land, perished in his attempt to escape from Robben Island; but now a man arises superior to all of these, who, after captivity of a few months, is liberated from Robben Island.

Passing over the effects likely to be produced on the powerful tribe of the Gaikas, with whom we were at war in 1835, 1846, and 1850, we have, across the Kei, the still more formidable tribe of Galekas under Kreli, the most powerful Chief on

our frontier, who forfeited a large portion of his country in 1858. This Chief is at present peaceful, because he sees no prospect of succeeding against us in war, but would not hesitate to join any powerful confederacy which held out any prospect of regaining his forfeited land and lost power. Kreli is regarded by the Gaikas as their Paramount Chief, and he exercises great influence over them as well as over other powerful tribes.

Six years since the Basutos, at the urgent request of their late Chief Moshesh became British subjects, and the tribe has ever since made rapid strides in civilization. But since the death of Moshesh his sons are endeavouring to regain that power and influence over the tribe which Moshesh surrendered for his people's good.

Whatever Bishop Colenso (with reference to whom, I may remark, that many of the facts stated in his book recently printed are so distorted as to make his conclusions unreliable) says to the contrary, there is no doubt that overtures were made by Langalibalele to Molapo, and which were favourably received; and it is more than probable that had it not been for the prompt action taken by this Government, and the presence of an armed Colonial force on the scene, as well as the pursuit by a large force from Natal, that Langalibalele would have found an asylum with Molapo, and the most embarrassing and wide-spread complications would have been the result.

There are undoubtedly, tribes which sympathize with the Hlubis, and regard their fate with grief and consternation, inasmuch as they have thus lost a powerful alliance, with the further result that the fate of Langalibalele has caused others to pause lest they should be placed in the same position.

The liberation of Langalibalele would produce the most serious consequences. By it the work of civilization, under our rule now so satisfactorily progressing, would be checked and retarded; the disaffected would be strengthened; the wavering would be gained by the disaffected; and the evil consequences which may result cannot be foreseen. It cannot be forgotten that the most disastrous war we have experienced, that of 1850-53 was brought about by the agency of a magician; and that in 1856, the bold and reckless attempt of Kreli to drive the Kafirs to desperation in a combined attack on the Colony, by causing the destruction of their cattle and their means of subsistence, was brought about by the agency of the prophet Umhlakaza. Langalibalele may have more power

and influence than either of the two through whom so much evil was wrought. He has long been famous with the Zulus and other tribes on the borders of Natal; late proceedings have brought him to note with tribes who knew little of him; his liberation from well-merited captivity would give him immense importance in the eyes even of the well-disposed, and would so greatly magnify his position that he would be most enthusiastically received wherever he went; and the ovations with which he would be met would so inflate him as to lead him to actions the results of which might be most disastrous.

(Signed)   C. BROWNLEE,
          Secretary for Native Affairs.
Office of the Secretary for Native Affairs, Cape Town, January, 1875.

WEENEN COUNTY.

On Wednesday last [17 February 1875], a meeting was held at Estcourt, when the following address to the Governor was adopted. . . .
To His Excellency Sir Benjamin Chilley Campbell Pine, K.C.M.G., &c., &c., &c., Lieutenant-Governor of Natal.

Sir,—We, the undersigned, inhabitants of the County of Weenen Natal, have learned with deep regret that you have been re-called from your Government, as believed by the Native and European races, on account of the prompt measures which you used in preventing the spread and punishing the insurrection of Langalibalele and his tribe.

It must be matter of satisfaction to Your Excellency to find that your conduct in these difficult circumstances meets with the warm and all but universal approval of the inhabitants of Natal, the Cape Colony, the Free State, and the Transvaal,—who, from their intimate knowledge of Kafir character, and Kafir affairs, are the best qualified to form correct opinions on the true nature of such insurrectionary movements, on the necessity of immediate action to prevent loss of life and property, and on the danger of dallying with such proceedings.

Believing this, we, the undersigned, inhabitants of the County of Weenen,— the scene of this revolt against lawful authority,—feel especially called upon to come forward to assure Your Excellency of our sincere gratitude for the responsibility you took upon yourself, and for the successful manner in which you met and put down this revolt, with the assistance of the Cape authorities, before it had time to become general.

We look upon your successful settlement of this long-intended outbreak as having secured the peace of this colony. From our knowledge of Kafir character, we can say, that delay or vacillation on the part of Your Excellency would have been fraught with disaster, have led to other tribes becoming involved, and so increased the difficulty of putting down the rebellion, as to have rendered large assistance from Her Majesty's Government absolutely essential.

Where your conduct of affairs deserved on all hands the highest commendation, it is to us matter of profound regret to find, that the responsibility you undertook, alike in the interest of the Crown, and of both races in this Colony, and the successful issue, without cost to the Imperial Treasury to which you brought these necessary operations, have been so little understood and appreciated by the Home Authorities. We feel assured that many, who in ignorance of our position and the facts of the case, have been even induced to believe in our enslaving women and children, and in the induction of a cruelty and injustice which never took place, will, at some future time admit their own misconceptions, and do justice to Your Excellency and ourselves.

Error may have been committed by Your Excellency's Government in not putting on evidence at the trial of these rebels, many important facts which would have shown more completely to Her Majesty's Ministers the true character of the circumstances and the population you had to deal with in this colony on your arrival here—a state of things which we have long been aware of, and which we saw must, sooner or later, result in anarchy and confusion.

With a Native Policy, said to have been dictated by the Imperial Government, possessed of deficient information, and carried out against the remonstrances and better knowledge of the Legislative Council and the people, native revolt was but a question of time.

Probably Your Excellency was so clearly convinced of the nature and meaning of Langalibalele and Putili's conduct, and of the extent of their criminality, that you took it for granted that a long continuance of criminal action—which could only have one meaning, and lead only to one result—would be apparent to people at a distance, as it was to those on the spot, and that your report that you found things so would be accepted as correct. The result shows that it was not so, and that the absence of such evidence has given room to challenge the fairness of your decision, and to create the opinion among those ignorant of all the circumstances, that the punishment of the rebels has been greater than they deserved.

We allude to such facts, for example, as the following, shewing the real character and conduct of these chiefs and their tribes:—

1. That on the flight of Langalibalele and his tribe, accompanied by his relative, Putili, into this colony in 1849, he arbitrarily settled himself in a location, which by its proximity to the power he fled from was an invitation to invasion;

and on being remonstrated with by the Government, refused to remove, and did not, in fact, remove, until compelled to do so by an armed force sent against him by this Government.

2. The warning given to Government by the Magistrate of this County, several years ago, that the conduct of Langalibalele and his people caused him increasing uneasiness and anxiety, and that if disturbance to the public peace occurred in Weenen County, he had reason to believe these people would be deeply concerned in it.

3. This Chief's conduct at the meeting at Estcourt in 1869, with reference to his wholesale evasion of the Marriage Law, and defrauding Government of the fees due under it—a law which he pretended not to understand, although he was one of those who had asked for it, in preference to an increase of the annual hut-tax—conduct which compelled the Secretary for Native Affairs, in the hearing of the whole meeting, including messengers from other tribes who attended to see how the matter would end, to warn him and his councillors that the contumacy he habitually displayed was such, that if persisted in would infallibly draw upon himself and his tribe severe censure, and condign punishment from the British Government.

4. The meetings of Langalibalele and his people in their location, where the propriety of obeying the orders of Government was discussed, at which the old men counselled obedience to Government, while Langalibalele and the young men resolved to disobey.

5. The training and armed drills of the men of the tribe, and their practicing in their location, with firearms, of which they were illegally possessed.

6. The storing of fastnesses in the mountains behind their location with grain, indicative of preparation for war.

7. The sprinkling or anointing of the men preparatory to warlike or predatory operations, some weeks after the feast and sprinkling for the First-fruits, which took place at the usual time.

8. The threats of some of the tribe to settlers in this county, and such statements as that they need no longer cultivate the soil, because before long Langalibalele would expel the white people, and take possession of their property.

9. The finding of large numbers of stolen horses and cattle in their location, in many cases even marked with white men's brands.

10. The stoppage by the Free State Authorities of large parties of Langalibalele's people marching armed through the Free State, to assist their tribe in Natal.

11. The large meeting with Putili in his location in the winter of 1873 to advise him to arm his tribe; "to be prepared for the time that was coming;" and to send his young men to the Diamond Fields as labourers to buy guns there, which they could introduce into their location under cloud of night; that he (Langalibalele) was doing so with his young men.

12. The withdrawal of members of Langalibalele's tribe who had refused to join in the revolt, into places of concealment, and the warnings some of the old men gave to the white inhabitants to be on their guard, and to remove from their homesteads with their live stock, because now that Langalibalele was safe himself over the mountain with most of his cattle and horses, he would send back commandos of his young men to slay, steal, and burn, as he had done

in former days on his flight from Zulu Country into this Colony.

13. Thefts of horses and cattle at the time of the flight over the mountain from settlers in the neighbourhood of the location, and thereafter the forcing open and robbing of homesteads.

14. In addition to a message sent to loyal members of his tribe, the messages sent to some small tribes threatening them also with destruction, if they refused to assist him.

15. The messages sent to larger tribes, asking them to join in defying the white man's Government, such, for example, as to that of Kukulele, who at one time agreed to assist, but on the advice of his uncle and some of the old men, afterwards refused to do so.

16. The messages and intrigues with the different tribes beyond the boundary to the South and West, some of which were discovered and communicated to your Government by the authorities of the Cape Colony months previous to the commencement of hostilities here. The treasonable proceedings referred to also in the report of Mr. Orpen, the Chief Magistrate, Tsitsa, dated March, 1874.

17. The messages and intrigues with Cetywayo, the King of the Zulus, on our northern and eastern boundaries.

18. The refusal of Putili and his tribe to assist Government with commissariat cattle, although bound by law to do so.

19. Their harbouring of Langalibalele's cattle and people in large numbers.

20. Their deceiving their Magistrate by sending to complain that their conduct was misrepresented to Government, and stating that they neither had any of Langalibalele's cattle nor people in their location, nor had had any friendly communications with them.

21. The finding some of Langalibalele's people and some of his family, large numbers of his cattle, and upwards of 200 stand of arms, illegally in their possession, in their location, when surrounded and the tribe disarmed.

22. That many of the young men of Putili's tribe on this occasion were absent from the location; that their absence was not accounted for by the old men when enquired into; that some were afterwards seen herding Langalibalele's cattle, and some were found in the ranks of his forces when they surrendered in the Basuto country.

23. That when, as a last attempt to bring these people back to their duty, proclamation was made desiring all who were loyal to Government to come out and separate themselves from the rebels, few or none did so, but determined to resist the Government, they deserted the women and children of their tribe, so as not to be encumbered with their presence, and left them on the hands of the Local Government, to be protected and fed at the expense of the colony.

We are well aware of the persistent and successful action of these people in concealing all such matters from their Magistrate and the Government at the time of their occurrence; and of the absence of a system of detective police in this colony. We are also aware that in similar circumstances a course of concealment was often unsuccessfully practised in former years against the Government of the Cape Colony. But still, after the revolt was put down, and before the trial of the prisoners, most if not all of these facts became gradually known to the public, and began to be talked of.

We are of the opinion that if such facts as the above, now well known, had upon the trial been carefully sifted, patiently inquired into, and put on record, the difficulties and dangers Your Excellency found existing in this colony on your arrival, would have been apparent. It would have been seen that these were not the result of a sudden, unpremeditated impulse, but of a long-contemplated attempt to set the authority of Government at defiance, with the assistance of other tribes. Your position, and the necessity of your action, would have been better understood by the Home Government, and we should have been spared the humiliation of seeing a portion of the Press and the people of our Mother Country condemning unheard their fellow-subjects in this colony, on the superficial and distorted evidence presented to them from various extraneous and partially-informed sources.

With scarcely one exception, it has been assumed by the English Press that the Kafir population of Natal is a native one, possessed of birthrights to the soil and British protection; whereas the fact and the truth is that the vast bulk of the Kafirs inhabiting the colony, and universally, with but one exception, those who have hitherto been a source of trouble to the local authorities, are refugees from neighbouring tribes who have settled in Natal, induced thereto by the justice and general kindness of the colonists to the native.

We call attention to the remarkable fact that in a country where, as is well known, religious differences have prevailed with more than ordinary violence, Ministers of the Gospel of all denominations — Episcopalian, Presbyterian, Wesleyan, Independent, Baptist, and Lutheran —and of different nationalities, have combined to place solemnly upon record their approval of the necessity, moderation, justice, and humanity of your proceedings.

Among these reverend gentlemen will be found the names of upwards of twenty men who have for many years conducted large missionary undertakings in the midst of the natives—speaking their language, consulted by them, thoroughly understanding their every act and symbol, and who have on all occasions hitherto shown themselves to be the friends and protectors of the natives.

When we consider the professional and social position, and the number of these gentlemen, it is a matter of some surprise to us that testimony of such apparent and real value, should not have been accepted in preference to the questionable evidence produced at home, and which it was impossible for the colonists at that time to reject or deny.

It is scarcely possible within the limits of this address, to expose in minute detail, calumnies circulated against yourself and the colony; but we trust we have said enough to justify ourselves, not only in our expressions of confidence and gratitude towards Your Excellency, and in our resolve to share, so far as that is possible, the responsibilities you have undertaken on behalf of this colony and of the British Empire of which it forms a portion, but also to induce those who may hitherto have been led by *ex parte* statements to form crude and hasty conclusions, to re-consider the grounds of their verdict against colonists who are as true to the instincts and traditions of Englishmen as are the men who remain in England.

We deeply regret that Your

Excellency's term of office in Natal, to which we all looked forward with such bright anticipations, should have proved a season fraught with so much of anxiety, trouble and disappointment, and that your actions have met in the Mother Country with no other return than misrepresentation and misconstruction.

Bearing in mind the many appropriate and valuable measures Your Excellency introduced during your former administration of this country, and likewise since you resumed its Government, we look upon your Excellency's recall as singularly inopportune; we consider it most unfortunate in the interests of both races inhabiting this colony, as occurring immediately after the release of Langalibalele, universally regarded by the natives as an evidence of weakness, and an encouragement to armed resistance to the Local Government, and by the European population as a total disregard of the interests of the colony, and a condemnation of acts essentially necessary for their preservation.

We sincerely trust that you will find at home that complete restoration to perfect health, and that rest, which have been denied you in this country.

We have the honour to be,
Your Excellency's grateful friends
and obedient servants,
Estcourt, Weenen County, Feb.,
1875.

The Victoria Cross Heroes of Rorke's Drift

CHARD, Lieutenant JOHN ROUSE MERRIOTT, Royal Engineers (No. 5 Company).

Born at Boshill, near Plymouth, on 21 December 1847, the son of W. W. Chard, of Pathe, Somerset, and Mount Tamar, Devon. Educated at Plymouth New Grammar School, Cheltenham College, and the Royal Military Academy, Woolwich. Entered the Royal Engineers 15 July 1868. Stationed for a time in Bermuda, later went to South Africa at the outbreak of the Zulu War. As a few months senior to Lieutenant Bromhead, he took command of the garrison of Rorke's Drift. In the Defence he was not wounded and assisted by Schiess as depicted in the film *Zulu* but succumbed to fever afterwards, and went to Ladysmith to recover. He took part in the Battle of Ulundi on 4 July 1879. Promoted Captain and Brevet Major for the Defence of Rorke's Drift, he was awarded the V.C., being decorated by H.E. Lieutenant-General Sir Garnet J. Wolseley, G.C.M.G., K.C.B., then G.O.C. and Governor of Natal. The ceremony took place at St Paul's Mission Station near Inkwenke Camp, Natal, on 16 July 1879. In his Journal Wolseley gave a very poor opinion of Chard as an officer; indeed he also disparaged the importance of the Defence of Rorke's Drift.

Chard left South Africa for England. At Plymouth he was presented with a telegram from H.M. Queen Victoria, who received him at Balmoral. He was never employed again and retired as Colonel in August 1897. He died at Hatch Beauchamp Rectory, near Taunton, on 1 November 1897, and was buried in the churchyard there on 5 November. He was within two months of reaching the age of fifty. His V.C. and medals are with his great-nephew; but a duplicate V.C., formerly in the possession of the late Sir Stanley Baker, is now with a collector in Canada.

BROMHEAD, Lieutenant Gonville, 2nd/24th (2nd Warwickshire) Regiment.

Born 29 August 1844 at Versailles, France; third son of Sir Edmund de Gonville Bromhead, Bt, of Thurlby, Lincolnshire, and Judith Christine, daughter of James Wood, Esq., of Woodville, Sligo. His name Gonville derived from the founder of Gonville College, Cambridge. He was educated at Newark, and joined the 24th (2nd Warwickshire) Regiment as an Ensign on 20 April 1867; nevertheless Chard who joined the Royal Engineers in 1868 was slightly senior to him in substantive rank. Bromhead was in command of B Company of his Regiment and, left behind by Lord Chelmsford to protect the Drift, was handicapped by being extremely deaf. He was mentioned in Despatches, awarded the V.C., and promoted Captain and Brevet Major for his services in the Defence. While Chelmsford loudly praised the excellent services of these two officers under the most trying circumstances, conducting the Defence with intelligence and tenacity, H.E. Lieutenant-General Sir Garnet J. Wolseley, who had no great opinion of Chelmsford, showed similar bias against the intelligence of both Bromhead and Chard. In his Journal he writes 'gave away the Victoria X' to those recipients he decorated. He decorated Brevet Major Bromhead at Utrecht, Natal, on 11 September 1879.

Major Bromhead served in the Burmese Expeditions of 1885 and 1887-80, receiving the Medal with two Clasps. His death took place at Allahabad, India, on 9 February 1891 at the early age of forty-six and six months. His V.C. and Medals, formerly with his grandnephew, were in 1973 bequeathed to the Regimental Museum of the South Wales Borderers at Brecon.

ALLAN, 1240 Corporal WILLIAM WILSON, 2nd/24th (2nd Warwickshire) Regiment.

Allan, whose name is frequently mis-spelt Allen, was born in 1844. His V.C. was gazetted 2 May 1879 for his gallant conduct in enabling the patients being withdrawn from the Hospital, being severely wounded in so doing. His excellent marksmanship on that occasion and subsequently in peacetime, earned for him the appointment of Sergeant-Instructor of Musketry. He was decorated by Her Majesty Queen Victoria in the Corridor of Windsor Castle on 9 December 1879. He died at Monnow Street, Monmouth, on 12 March 1890, aged forty-six, and was buried at Monmouth.

His V.C. and Medals were purchased on 21 June 1906 by Philip A. Wilkins, and they are now in the Regimental Museum of the South Wales Borderers at Brecon.

DALTON, JAMES LANGLEY, Acting Assistant Commissary, Commissariat and Transport Department.

Born in St Andrew's Parish, London, in December 1832, Langley had worked in a stationer's shop before enlisting on 21 November 1849 at the age of seventeen years and eleven months in the 85th Regiment. This regiment was known at the time as 'The Bucks Volunteers', and from 1821 'The King's Light Infantry'. In 1881 the Cardwell reorganization renamed it the 2nd Battalion the King's Shropshire Infantry. Dalton served in Mauritius, Canada, and the Cape of Good Hope, where he was stationed for five and a half years, taking part in the Eighth Frontier War of 1850-53. He attained the rank of Sergeant, and then transferred to the Commissariat and Transport Department. In February 1866 he was promoted to Quartermaster-Sergeant. On 9 November 1871 he took his discharge, being pensioned and awarded the Long Service and Good Conduct Medal. He returned to South Africa to settle in Natal. He volunteered at the outbreak of the Ninth Frontier War and was given the temporary appointment of Assistant Commissary on 13 December 1877. For his energetic services rendered at the Ibeka Headquarters he was thanked by Major-General Sir Arthur Cunynghame, K.C.B. The imminent danger of the Zulu threat caused him to return to Natal to join General Thesiger's forces. He was placed second in command of the Field Depot at Rorke's Drift. Having passed a course in field fortifications, the services of this veteran soldier proved invaluable to Chard and Bromhead. It was generally considered that it was he who was most responsible for devising the defences. His services having been overlooked in the *London Gazette* of 2 May pressure of public opinion caused questions to be asked in Parliament. The omission was rectified by the award gazetted on 17 November 1879. The citation enumerated his acts of gallantry. An expert marksman, he inflicted heavy losses on the Zulus at the corner of the Hospital. One Zulu who had sprung on to the barricade, seized the rifle of a private and was about to assegai him, when Dalton rushed forward and saved the man's life by shooting his assailant. Dalton was severely wounded in the back by a shot fired from the terrace of the Oscarberg. Nevertheless, he remained at his post until after the enemy had retired. He was decorated by Wolseley's successor, Major-General The Hon. Henry Hugh Clifford, V.C., C.B., at Fort Napier, Maritzburg, Natal in 1880. He died at the Grosvenor Hotel, Port Elizabeth, on 8 January 1887, aged fifty-four, and was buried in the Russell Road Cemetery there.

AUTHOR'S NOTE

I have to thank Major G. J. B. Egerton, D.L., Curator of the Regimental Museum at Brecon, for checking the records of the men of the 24th Regiment.

HITCH, 1362 Private FREDERICK, 2nd/24th (2nd Warwickshire) Regiment.

Hitch was born at New Southgate, Middlesex, on 28 November 1856. He had little schooling, for he was aged fourteen when the Act of 1870 enforced compulsory education. He enlisted in the 24th Regiment and served through the Kaffir War of 1877-78. He and Corporal Allan together held open the communication between the Hospital and the Inner Defence, thus enabling the wounded to be carried across when the Zulus set light to the thatched building. Previous to this he had been sent by Bromhead to climb up to the ridge-pole of the Hospital to get a clear view of the western flank of the Oscarberg. On the arrival of the Zulus, Hitch came down from the roof and joined the defenders along the front wall. Allan was wounded in the arm, but Hitch was more greatly disabled by a slug which smashed into his shoulder, making a nasty gash, and shattering the shoulder-blade to pieces. He rolled over to the centre of the yard and crawled to the wall of the Hospital where he sat beside Allan. The two men assisted the patients as they dropped from the window, Hitch using his good arm, the other hanging useless. Dr Reynolds attended to him and extracted thirty-six pieces of his shoulder-blade before sewing him up. Yet he continued to serve out ammunition to his comrades after that. He was invalided to England, where in Netley Hospital, Her Majesty Queen Victoria pinned the Cross on his breast on 12 August 1879.

After discharge from the Army he held various positions of responsibility, and as a member of the Corps of Commissionaires was on duty at the Imperial Institute and the Royal United Service Institution, Whitehall.

While at the R.U.S.I., he had the misfortune to have his Cross stolen from his jacket. On the order of King Edward VII it was replaced by a duplicate, which was presented to him by King Edward VII at the request of Hitch in 1908. This Cross was sold on 21 November 1929 and passed into the possession of the Regimental Museum of the South Wales Borderers at Brecon.

In his later years Hitch was a London cab-driver, and was the owner of two horses. He died at 62 Cranbrook Road, Chiswick, London on 7 January 1913 aged fifty-six years. His body was buried in Chiswick Cemetery on 11 January.

HOOK, 1373 Private HENRY ALFRED, 2nd/24th (2nd Warwickshire) Regiment.

Hook was born at Churcham in Gloucestershire in May 1850. He served five years in the Monmouthshire Militia before joining the 24th

Regiment. He, too, served throughout the Kaffir War of 1877-78. He and John and Joseph Williams, together with Private William Horrigan of the 1st Battalion, held the distant room in the Hospital for a full hour, as long as their ammunition lasted. The Zulus burst open the door and dragged out Joseph Williams and two patients, and assegaied them. Hook, who had been detailed as a cook for the Hospital, posted himself in a corner room with Private Thomas Cole, a gigantic man, popularly known as 'Old King Cole'. These two barricaded the back door with mealie bags. They knocked a hole in the side wall and another in the rear wall. Cole left the room to join the men on the front barricade, leaving Hook to defend the end two rooms alone. Cole was subsequently killed by a bullet through the head. Hook and John Williams safely passed eight patients through a small window into the inner line of defence. Private Hook was decorated with the V.C. by H.E. Lieutenant-General Sir Garnet J. Wolseley, G.C.M.G., K.C.B., on 3 August 1879 at Fort Melvill, Rorke's Drift being one of the few recipients decorated on the scene of their exploits.

He served in the 1st Volunteer Battalion of the Royal Fusiliers as a Sergeant. For some years he was on the staff of the British Museum. Dying at his native village of Churcham on 12 March 1905, he was buried in the churchyard there on 18 March. I met his married daughter Mrs Bunting as a spectator of the V.C. Centenary Review on 26 June 1956, and she gave me a photograph of her father and stated his correct Christian names in their proper order but I have retained the official nomenclature. His V.C. is one of the Rorke's Drift Crosses now in the Regimental Museum of the South Wales Borderers at Brecon.

JONES, 716 Private ROBERT, 2nd/24th (2nd Warwickshire) Regiment.

Jones was born at Raglan, Monmouthshire, on 19 August 1857. He enlisted in the 24th Regiment about August 1875, joining the 2nd Battalion at Dover at the end of 1876. He and the much older William Jones barricaded themselves in the Hospital and evacuated about six patients through the small window, which they enlarged by knocking out the frame with an axe. All the patients reached the enclosure in safety; but Sergeant Maxfield, who was delirious, refused to go. After William Jones had lifted Private Connolly to the window and lowered him to the ground, he turned back to find Sergeant Maxfield in the smoke-filled room. He was too late, the Zulus had broken through and killed him. He scrambled back out of the window as the roof collapsed behind him, and made his way to the enclosure.

Robert Jones was decorated at the same time as Major Bromhead by H.E. Lieutenant-General Sir Garnet J. Wolseley, G.C.M.G., K.C.B. at

Utrecht, Natal, on 11 September 1879. There is some doubt as to where he died. Philip Wilkins states that he died in London; Creagh and Humphris say Madley, Hereford, on 6 September 1898; but Prebendary Beattie, Rector of Madley, and father of Captain S. Beattie, V.C., R.N., contradicts this. Anyway he was buried in Peterchurch Graveyard, Herefordshire. He was aged forty-one. His V.C. was in the possession of the late Mr Charles H. Lovell, M.B.E., Royal Gloucestershire Hussars, Cirencester, who died on 6 May 1977. His collection of five V.C.s and hundreds of other medals was sold at Glendining's on 12 June 1952 and 5 March 1969. The remainder of Lovell's collection was sold at Sothebys on 22 and 23 November 1977. The V.C. is now owned by a Mr Hughes of Somerset.

JONES, 593 Private WILLIAM, 2nd/24th (2nd Warwickshire) Regiment.

Jones was born in Bristol in 1840. Distinguished from his younger comrade by a black goatee beard he was associated with him in the extrication of the patients from the Hospital against tremendous odds. He received his V.C. at the hands of Her Majesty Queen Victoria at Windsor Castle on 13 January 1880. He was discharged from the Army Reserve on 26 January 1888. I find no record of his civilian life. His death occurred at 6 Brampton Street, Ardwick, Lancashire on 15 April 1913 at the age of seventy-three. His remains were interred in Bradford Cemetery, Manchester, on 21 April. The Regimental Museum of the South Wales Borderers has his V.C. at Brecon.

REYNOLDS, Surgeon-Major JAMES HENRY, Army Medical Department, attached 2nd/24th (2nd Warwickshire) Regiment.

His V.C. was gazetted on 17 June 1879, seven weeks after the first awards for Rorke's Drift. He was the son of Mr L. Reynolds, J.P., of Dalyston House, Granard, Ireland and was born at Kingstown, Dublin on 3 February 1844. Educated at Castle Knock, and Trinity College, Dublin, where he graduated B.A. and Hon.LL.D., he entered the Medical Staff Corps as Assistant-Surgeon on 31 March 1868; becoming Surgeon on 1 March 1873. He had seen service in the Perie Bush and was now in charge of the Field Hospital at Rorke's Drift with three men of the Army Hospital Corps to help him and Private Hook of the 24th as cook. Reynolds utilized the building erected by Rorke the settler and which Otto Witt, the Swedish missionary, had made his residence. It was a poor building, but Reynolds made the best use he could of it. His patients were crammed into three small rooms and three cubbyholes, four of which had each their own door at the side or back of the building. Hook had to use a small shanty and a few outside ovens for cooking. These were behind the storehouse, formerly the mission chapel. Artillery-fire having been heard from a distance Surgeon Reynolds, with the Swedish missionary Otto Witt and the Reverend George Smith (Chaplain), and Private Wall, climbed the Oscarberg to find out the reason. Reynolds was the first to descend when he heard the approach of the first two men in flight from Isandhlwana, as he thought there might be need of his medical attendance. When at length the Zulus arrived the use of his little accommodation as a hospital was out of the question and he attended the wounded out in the open in the light of the burning building. Here he was kept busy under cross-fire throughout the night. His promotion to Surgeon-Major for distinguished field service was dated 23 January 1879. His V.C. he received from H.E. Lieutenant-General Sir Garnet Wolseley, G.C.M.G., K.C.B., on 26 August. He was present at Ulundi on 4 July 1879. Besides the V.C. he was awarded the South African Medal with three dates—1877, 1878, 1879—and for Rorke's Drift the Gold Medal of the British Medical Association. He joined the 36th (Herefordshire) Regiment in 1869 in Bengal. For services rendered during a severe outbreak of cholera in the 36th Regiment in India, he received the approbation of the Commander-in-Chief, Lord Sandhurst. His subsequent steps in promotion were to Lieutenant-Colonel on 1 April 1887 and Brigade-Surgeon Lieutenant-Colonel on 25 December 1892. He retired in 1896 and later was in medical charge of the Royal Army Clothing Factory, Pimlico. He married Elizabeth, daughter of Dr McCormick in 1880. His death occurred at Haslemere, Surrey on 4 March 1932, a month after his eighty-eighth birthday. He was buried at Haslemere on 9 March. Pictures of him at Rorke's Drift winning his V.C. are to be found at the Headquarters of the Royal Army Medical Corps at Millbank in London. His Victoria Cross and medals probably remain with his family.

SCHIESS, 138 Corporal CHRISTIAN FERDINAND, 3rd Natal Native Contingent.

The only man of Swiss birth to be awarded the Victoria Cross. He was born at Bergdorf, Canton Berne, on 7 April 1856, and named at baptism Christian Ferdinand. These names apparently became an embarrassment to him, for in after life he went by the name of Friederich, and as such appeared in official documents and published accounts about him. His father was Niklaus Schiess, a humble stone-cutter, known as 'Bernese Schiess', who was born at Oberburg, Canton Berne, on 12 March 1820, and died in the Municipal Asylum, Herisau, on 21 September 1893. His mother, Anna Schiess (née Ruchti) was born on 19 February 1820 at Munchen-Buchese, Canton Berne, and died on 3 November 1863. On her death young Schiess and his father entered the Municipal Orphanage at Herisau, Canton Appenzell.

He left the orphanage in his fifteenth year and served for five and a half years in the French Army (1871-76) being under General Bourbaki's command at the end of the Franco-Prussian War. This army in defeat became interned in Switzerland. I have the names of those who were thus kept prisoners of war in Herisau. It would be ironical to think of Schiess being interned in his native country, but all efforts to ascertain the title of the regiment or regiments in which he served proved futile. Le Ministre d'Etat Chargé de la Defense Nationale writes to me: 'Monsieur, J'ai l'honneur de vous faire connaitre que les recherches concernant Christian Ferdinand Schiess restées infructueuses.' A similar inquiry through Lord Gladwyn of the Archives of the French Foreign Legion also proved fruitless. One can only think that Schiess used an assumed name.

His service terminated, he emigrated to South Africa about July 1876. There as an unskilled itinerant labourer he wandered about for about two and a half years until caught up in the Kaffir Wars. His exploits in these were legendary, but not being recorded on paper they cannot be related here. His gigantic stature and his ability as a leader of men caused him to be picked by Colonel A. W. Durnford for the newly organized Natal Native Contingent, the conception of General Thesiger, afterwards Lord Chelmsford. Thus Schiess became a Corporal in the 3rd Natal Native Contingent, and saw service at the taking of Sihayo's kraal on 11 January 1879. Here he was wounded in the calf by an assegai and Corporal Mayer, N.N.C., received a wound behind the knee on the same occasion. The two N.C.O.s, together with a captured Zulu, found themselves in the little Hospital at Rorke's Drift and so played their parts in its defence. The Zulu unfortunately was killed by his fellow countrymen in the Hospital.

No photograph was ever taken of Schiess, but the film Zulu portrays appropriately his burly frame in the uniform of what may be that of Lonsdale's Horse which he later joined. In the film he is seen telling young Henry Hook about the running powers and the fighting ability of the Zulus. Later, Schiess is shown running from the Hospital to take his part in the defence of the barrier, the bandage on his leg loosening on the way. In the paintings by De Neuville and Lady Butler he is depicted, truthfully, as wearing a slouch hat with the N.N.C. red band, and standing on the mealie bags bayoneting the enemy. One Zulu creeping up to the barricade closely discharged his rifle at him. The blast blew the hat off. Schiess slew the Zulu, jumped down, retrieved his hat and was back on the barricade in time to dispatch another warrior clambering up and yet a third in his frenzy. These acts won him the V.C.

After Rorke's Drift the unsatisfactory Natal Native Contingent was disbanded. Many of its members had fled from the field of Isandhlwana as so, too, had those at Rorke's Drift before the Zulus arrived. Their European officers and men joined other irregular units. Thus Corporal Schiess was transferred to Lonsdale's Horse, in the green uniform of which he appeared, to be given a public ovation when introduced by Lonsdale in a speech describing his career. It was at this ceremony in Market Square, Pietermaritzburg, on 3 February 1880, that Colonel Brackenbury read the letter from Colonel Stanley, the Secretary of State for War to H.E. Lieutenant-General Sir Garnet J. Wolseley, G.C.M.G., K.C.B., giving the command of Her Majesty the Queen for him to present the Victoria Cross to Corporal Schiess followed by the citation in the *London Gazette* of 20 November 1879. The General made a long speech, shook hands with Schiess, and as he pinned the Cross on his breast said: 'I hope you will live very long indeed to wear the decoration.'

Alas! that wish was not fulfilled. The last five years of the Corporal's life were tragic. He became very ill and stricken with poverty in King Williamstown and was invalided to England. A passage was found for him on the troopship *Serapis*, friends paying for his food. He never reached England. The Captain's log of H.M.S. *Serapis* (ADM/53/15678) in the Public Record Office reads:

Sunday, 14th December, 1884:
10.20 a.m. Departed this life Mr. F. C. SCHIESS, VC
5.10 p.m. Stopped. Committed to the Deep the remains of the late Mr SCHIESS, VC
5.15 Proceeded
Ship's Noon observed Position: Lat S. 13.00: Long W. 7.24

I make this position about 360 statute miles west of the coast of Angola, and 830 statute miles east-north-east of the Island of St Helena.

In spite of his ill fortune Schiess had not parted with his precious Victoria Cross; but, being a single man, there was no next of kin to claim it. Hence it passed to the War Office, where it was kept in a drawer for many years. Then when the National Army Museum was formed at the Royal Military College, Sandhurst, it was sent there. It was given a case to itself along with a Zulu shield and assegai. It was transferred to the new museum at Chelsea, where it can be seen today. Near it is a model of Rorke's Drift and its garrison, among whom may be seen a khaki-clad figure wearing a slouch hat with a red band in the centre of the enclosure.

At his death 'Friederich' Schiess was twenty-eight years and eight months, the youngest of the Rorke's Drift V.C.s and its most tragic member.

For details of his boyhood and his ancestry I am greatly indebted to his distant kinsman, Mr Otto Schiess, of St Gallen.

Although the V.C. hero was born of humble parents, many of his ancestors played a distinguished part in Swiss history.

WILLIAMS, 1395 Private JOHN, 2nd/24th (2nd Warwickshire) Regiment.

Williams was born at Abergavenny, Monmouthshire, on 24 May 1857, his real name being John Williams Fielding. He was the son of a policeman who had a family of eight children. He ran away from home to enlist and took his second Christian name as a surname so that he should not be traced. He served through the Kaffir War of 1877-78. Together with Private Joseph Williams, whose regimental number 1398 indicates that both enlisted at the same time, he held the centre room of the Hospital at Rorke's Drift which at the time held five patients. One of these was Private W. Horrigan of the 1st Battalion, who was able to stand. The three men barricaded the flimsy door as best they could and knocked three holes in the wall through which to shoot. Finding a pickaxe John Williams knelt between two patients and in the cramped space managed to enlarge his loophole in the wall, while the other Williams and Horrigan guarded the other two loopholes. Later Joseph Williams left his loophole and tried to stop it with his body, while John Williams wriggled through. John Williams dragged two patients through the narrow passage. Then the Zulus broke through the outside door and Joseph Williams was exposed to them. He bayoneted one of the enemy, and stabbed at others. The Zulus fell back and he reloaded his rifle. Fighting stoutly he held a dozen warriors back until one of them took hold of the barrel of his rifle. He tried to wrench the gun away, but the Zulus felled him, tore open his tunic, and ripped his body. They tore his corpse to pieces in their savagery. John Williams, when he turned, witnessed the horrible tragedy. There is no doubt that Joseph Williams would have been awarded the V.C. for his exceptional gallantry had only his name appeared in the *London Gazette* coupled with the words: 'would have been recommended for the Victoria Cross had he survived.'

John Williams survived to be decorated by Major-General Anderson, G.O.C. and C.-in-C. Gibraltar, on the Almeda Parade Ground, Gibraltar, on 1 March 1880. In civilian life he worked in a nut and bolt factory and lived to see the end of the First World War for his death at Cwmbrae, Monmouth did not take place until 25 November 1932, at the age of seventy-five years and six months. He was buried in St Michael's Churchyard, Llantarnam. His V.C. is exhibited in the Regimental Museum of the South Wales Borderers at Brecon. He was the last V.C. survivor of Rorke's Drift.

Incidentally John Williams was the only Rorke's Drift V.C. to live to attend the first two important V.C. Reunions. The first was the Garden Party given by Their Majesties King George V and Queen Mary to V.C. Recipients at Buckingham Palace on 26 June 1920. There is a picture of him in *The Illustrated London News* featuring the event. Then on 9 November 1920 he was one of the V.C. heroes who were entertained by the British Legion to dinner at the House of Lords.

I have a photograph of him taken with Company Sergeant-Major John H. Williams, V.C., D.C.M., M.M. of the 10th (Service) Battalion South Wales Borderers, whose Cross was won at Villers-Outreaux in France, 7-8 October 1918, and who died 6 March 1953. His V.C. is also in the Regimental Museum of the South Wales Borderers at Brecon. The photograph is by Jackson of Brecon.

Bibliography

Browne, G. Hamilton, *A Lost Legionary in South Africa* (1880).

Chard, Lieutenant J. R. M., *Official Report of the Defence of Rorke's Drift* (25 January 1879).

Colenso, Right Reverend J. W. (Bishop of Maritzburg), *Langalibalele and the amaHlubi Tribe* (1874).

Coupland, Reginald, *Zulu Battlepiece—Isandhlwana* (1948).

Durnford, Edward, *Memoir of the late A. W. Durnford* (1882).

Fisher, Reverend A. C. P., C.F., *The King's Division Depot Lancashire, The Garrison Church of St Alban, Fulwood Barracks* (1963).

Furneaux, Rupert, *The Zulu War: Isandhlwana and Rorke's Drift* (1963).

Glover, Michael, *Rorke's Drift—A Victorian Epic* (1975).

Hagan, Gerald, *Dry Docking* (1975).

Haggard, Sir H. Rider, 'Rorke's Drift' *(The True Story Book*, edited by Andrew Melville).

Jackson, F. W. D., 'Isandhlwana - the Sources Re-examined', *Journal of the Society for Army Historical Research* (1965).

Lancashire Daily Post, 'Reverend George Smith's Obituary' (27 November and 2 December 1918).

Lummis, Canon W. M., *Corporal Schiess, the Swiss V.C.* (to be published).

Narrative of the Field Operations Connected with the Zulu War (Intelligence Branch, 1881).

Natal Government Gazette, The, 'Further Papers relating to the Kafir Outbreak in Natal' (6 April 1875).

Reynolds, Surgeon-Major Lieutenant-Colnel J. H., Diary (Report to C.O. on Rorke's Drift, 1879).

Riley, Reverend G. V., C.F., 'A Striking Figure of the Past' *(Royal Army Chaplains Department Journal*, 1918).

Society for the Propagation of the Gospel, Reports from Missionaries in Zululand, 1872 to 1879 (in Archives of U.S.P.G.).

Tylden, Major Geoffrey, ed., *The Rise of the Basuto* (1950).

Uys, Ian S., *For Valour—the Story of the Southern African Victorian Cross Heroes* (1973).

Whitton, F.E. 'Rorke's Drift (*Blackwood's Magazine*, 1934).

Wilkins, Philip A., *History of the Victoria Cross* (1904).

Index